MATT FREDERICK

A Meeting at The Crossroads: Robert Johnson and The Devil

First published by Chicken Feet Press 2022

Copyright © 2022 by Matt Frederick

All rights reserved. No part of this publication may be reproduced, stored or transmitted in any form or by any means, electronic, mechanical, photocopying, recording, scanning, or otherwise without written permission from the publisher. It is illegal to copy this book, post it to a website, or distribute it by any other means without permission.

Matt Frederick asserts the moral right to be identified as the author of this work.

Designations used by companies to distinguish their products are often claimed as trademarks. All brand names and product names used in this book and on its cover are trade names, service marks, trademarks and registered trademarks of their respective owners. The publishers and the book are not associated with any product or vendor mentioned in this book. None of the companies referenced within the book have endorsed the book.

First edition

ISBN: 978-0-6452436-0-4

This book was professionally typeset on Reedsy.
Find out more at reedsy.com

To all who've gone searching for The Crossroads

Contents

Acknowledgement	ii
Heading Down to the Crossroads	1
The Story of the Blues	4
The Life and Times of Robert Johnson	23
The Crossroads and The Blues Tradition	51
The God of the Crossroads	83
Conclusion	112
APPENDIX A: Discovering the Crossroads	114
APPENDIX B: A Listener's Guide to Robert Johnson	131
APPENDIX C: A Robert Johnson Timeline	138
REFERENCES	143

Acknowledgement

My deepest thanks to all the researchers who came before me and discovered the person behind the name on aging index cards.

Thanks to Amy and Adam for their support and patience while I worked on this book at often odd hours.

Thanks to the CWS group and friends for regular late night virtual chats. Special thanks to Nerine and Alex for their practical advice and support.

Special thanks are reserved for Melbourne blues scene, to all the artists, broadcasters and fans who have created a unique and special place for blues lovers. In particular, I would like to thank John and Elly for their encouragement and PBS 106.7fm for giving me the ongoing opportunity to share music with blues lovers in Melbourne and beyond.

Heading Down to the Crossroads

I first saw the Crossroads from the window of a bus, but it was not a Greyhound. You might think Greyhound can take you anywhere, but if you want to explore the land of the Mississippi blues, you've got to ride Delta.

Nursing a hangover and getting by on only a couple of hours' sleep, I'd hopped on the Greyhound at New Orleans, changed to Delta at Baton Rouge, ran into a guy I knew from the pub back home in Melbourne, and gradually got acquainted with the back roads of Mississippi that you can only get to know when you travel by bus. Pulling into Clarksdale, the bus unexpectedly went past the famous intersection that featured a sculpture of two crossed guitars, and, despite myself, my heart skipped a little beat. I knew it wasn't the real Crossroads, whatever that's supposed to be, but it represented a search I'd been on since I'd first discovered Robert Johnson's music as a teenager.

Through his recordings, Johnson's story had become part of my story, and by searching for him, I had been searching for a part of myself. I wasn't the first to go on this quest, and I sure wouldn't be the last. Hearing the music and story of Robert Johnson had awakened something in me, just as it had awakened something in the listeners who first heard him play live and on the jukebox, in the collectors who first discovered his 78s, in the '60s guitar gods who felt compelled to share his music with the world. Even without the story, his music is just that good. It grabs you and refuses to let go; it's simultaneously otherworldly and down to earth; it comes from a specific time and place, yet it speaks to people almost a century in time and thousands of miles from its origin. This is, as I told myself after hearing "Crossroad Blues" for the first time as a teenager, the real shit.

The album cover makes the claim clearly enough: *The King of the Delta Blues Singers*. Others could lay claim to the crown: Son House, perhaps, or Charley Patton, or maybe a more recent artist such as Big George Brock or Robert "Wolfman" Belfour. But in terms of fame and recognition, Johnson has surely earned the crown. From its origins in the Mississippi Delta, his music has spread around the world. I have heard Robert Johnson's music played and performed in backstreet Bangkok bars and trendy Tel Aviv cafés.

It's fair to say that, for many people, Robert Johnson *is* the blues, defining the image of the music and the people who play it. His life has set the template not only for the hard-traveling bluesman but for the live fast, die young performers of the rock 'n' roll era that followed. His life story has all the excitement of a typical rock 'n' roll biography, but with the added romance of going to the source of things, that this is the wellspring, the archetype through which we understand the stories of Jim Morrison, Janis Joplin, Amy Winehouse, and all the other members of the famed "27 Club." Beyond this, there is the lure of the occult and the smell of brimstone. This is a performer who was supposedly in league with the Devil himself, and both his worldwide fame and early death are consequences of a pact made with Satan at midnight at a lonesome Mississippi Delta crossroads.

Before we go any further, we need to make things plain: The story of Robert Johnson going down to the Crossroads to sell his soul to Ol' Scratch is a goddamn lie. It never happened. Things like this just plain don't happen. If you choose to believe that the Prince of Darkness himself physically manifested in rural Mississippi in the early twentieth century and offered an itinerant bluesman and street singer fame and musical prowess in exchange for his immortal soul, then more power to you. But for most of us, that's not the way the world works.

HEADING DOWN TO THE CROSSROADS

The story of the Crossroads is not the story of an event that can be located in space and time, just as the Crossroads is not a place that you can find on Google Maps. The Crossroads isn't a location or a happening; it's a state of being, a process of transformation. The story of the Crossroads is a myth, to be sure, but that doesn't make it a thing to pass by or disregard. Myths get told for a reason; they carry meaning and guide us toward greater truths. As we will discover, the story of the Crossroads is bigger than that of Robert Johnson, echoing African American folklore, diaspora religion, and ancient archetypes. To dismiss the Crossroads is to dismiss these truths. We certainly need to know the man Robert Johnson, and to know him as best we can, it is essential for us to clear the way of lies and untruths. But to dismiss the mythic element entirely is to leave us with only half the story.

When traveling along the back roads of Mississippi, as the sun goes down and the darkness rises, and the bus winds its way past yet another lonely Delta crossroads, even the hardened skeptic will find themselves wondering how much truth lies behind the myth. Check the church billboards by the highways, the hand-painted signs on the side roads, the bumper stickers on the passing cars, or scan through the AM stations, and you'll soon discover that the Devil is an authentic presence in the American South. He takes on many forms. The Devil can be a malevolent force, a tempter and an agent of the apocalypse. He can also be a Trickster, a figure who can be both the cause and target of ridicule.

As we explore the myth of Robert Johnson, we're going to meet the Devil up close, along with the bluesmen who walked with him side by side. We'll dig into the weird works of myth and the occult to find the sources of the story and uncover the meaning behind the myth that has traveled the world. We'll barrelhouse down by the riverside and walk down the lonely highways, searching for the answer to the question, "What happens at the Crossroads?"

The Story of the Blues

The blues tells a story. Every line of the blues has meaning.
  - John Lee Hooker

The blues comes out of pain and sorrow, but also immense joy. Blues is a feeling, as the song goes, but it is also so much more than that. It is the story of a culture, a musical form. It can be a way of talking, a way of dressing, a way of being. It comes from within African American culture; it can't be understood without reference to this culture, yet, as we shall see, it belongs to a subset who sit apart from this culture, who are defined by their separation. The bluesman is defined as much by who he is *not* as by who he *is*.

There's an apocryphal line you sometimes see circulated online, often attributed to Jimi Hendrix: "The blues are easy to play but hard to feel." The provenance of the quote is hard to trace, but that's beside the point. That the line gets repeated, quoted, and circulated tells us a lot about the music and what separates it from related styles such as rock 'n' roll and jazz. The essential elements of the blues are simple enough for even rank beginners to pick up the basics. Three chords, one scale, and you're on your way to performing "Sweet Home Chicago" for tips with the bar band. But what you're playing isn't quite the blues, not until you understand the nuances, the subtleties that let you express the depths of emotion that define a musical form whose very name is a synonym for an emotional state.

Many attempts to define blues music point to its typical AAB, twelve-bar structure, and a melodic sense built out of the pentatonic minor scale, with the addition of so-called "blue notes," such as the major third and flattened fifth, to create the "blues scale." This is okay as far as it goes. Follow these rules, and you'll play something that sounds *like* the blues, but you've got a few more steps to go before you play something that is, as the musician Mezz Mezzrow put it, *really* the blues.

The first thing we have to do is throw the twelve-bar structure out the window. The blues form is much more flexible than that. A quick survey through some of the most famous blues songs is enough to tell you that. Muddy Waters' "Hoochie Coochie Man" is based on a sixteen-bar form, Little Walter's "Key to the Highway" is an example of only the eight-bar blues, and John Lee Hooker's "Boogie Chillen" is little more than a repetitive groove that stays stubbornly on the tonic, giving the vaguest hint of a chord change.

We find ourselves on firmer ground when we turn our attention to rhythm and melody. The blues musician builds his groove with triplets, the "one-and-a" beat that gives us the shuffle of Chicago blues, the swing of New Orleans, and complex polyrhythms found in the Mississippi Delta and the nearby Mississippi Hill Country. Melodically, an emphasis is placed on microtones, the notes between the piano keys that exist outside of Western musical notation. These provide us with the so-called "blue notes," specific pitches that sit outside of Western ideas of harmony. Listen to the vocal slurs and slide guitar on any Muddy Waters record and you soon get it. Specific microtonal pitches, such as the slur between the major and minor third, are essential parts of the blues musician's vocabulary. Take away the microtones and the music sounds less, well, blue. Stepping outside of the scales gives the music a wider tonal palette, creating further ways to express emotion, to create tension and release, allowing the musician to better express that feeling we call the blues.

Even without the use of microtones, the blues defies Western ideas of music by blurring the lines between the major and minor keys. Even when a blues song's harmony fits into the major scale—building on the chords E, A, and B in the key of E, or A, D, and E in the key of A—the underlying melody will contain notes borrowed from the minor scale. This creates a vague sense of unease, as notes drift in and out of tonality and the ear hears the music pitching both major and minor.

To the unfamiliar ear, musicians like John Lee Hooker, Howlin' Wolf, and even Robert Johnson can seem downright primitive, sticking to narrow melodic and harmonic forms and consistently returning to stock phrases, but the emotional content is undeniable. Like Sam Phillips said when he first heard Howlin' Wolf sing, this is where the soul of man never dies. A blues performance lives or dies on how it hits you inside. Skilled instrumentalists like Stevie Ray Vaughan or Gary Clark Jr. may have performed feats of guitar pyrotechnics beyond mortal ken, but all this serves to add color to the artist's emotional palette rather than existing for its own sake.

We shouldn't take this to mean that the blues implies a lack of skill or technical prowess. Anyone who thinks this is the case is welcome to spend some serious listening time with some T-Bone Walker and Little Walter records. Blues musicians are highly skilled players, celebrated by their peers for their vocal and instrumental prowess, but the musical skill is there purely to serve a higher purpose. You won't find the measure of a blues performance in instrumental or vocal pyrotechnics; you've got to dig deeper, down into the emotional content communicated by the player.

It can be said that the blues came out of Africa but was not born in Africa. We can hear clear traces of the blues in music from the African continent, both modern and traditional, but to consider this of-a-kind with the blues would be doing a great disservice to both the African traditions and one of America's great contributions to world culture. Sounds similar to the blues can be heard in the music of Mali, the nomads of the Sahara, in Zanzibar, and even in the call to prayer heard five times a day in Islamic North Africa, but the blues itself, both the music and the story that comes with it, is distinctly American.

Traces of the music that became the blues can be found in the instruments of Africa. The *xalam* of Mali, for example, consists of a number of strings stretched over a resonating membrane and typically tuned to an open chord and is a clear antecedent of not just the banjo but of the open-chord guitar tunings favored by Delta blues guitarists. The *ngoni* harp also found in parts of West Africa features a similar construction and is typically used to pick out pentatonic melodies that even the untrained ear can recognize as being only a few steps removed from the blues.

The genesis of what became the blues can ultimately be found in the forced mass migration from Africa to the Americas during the trans-Atlantic slave trade. The Spanish and Portuguese settlers of the New World had been quick to import cheap slave labor to work in their colonies. As the New World colonies grew, so did the demand for cheap labor. The slave trade in what was to become the United States can be dated as early as 1619. America—the nation that prided itself as a land of freedom where it is "self-evident that all men are created equal"—found itself built on the backs of indentured servitude. Records are incomplete; however, it has been estimated that between six and seven million people were imported from Africa, either directly or via the Caribbean, to work as slaves until Congress outlawed the trade in 1808. Even then, the internal trade continued until the Emancipation Act of 1863.

This forced mass migration from the Old World to the New took place with no consideration as to the culture and traditions that the people had been taken from. Slaves were taken from all over the African continent, from what we now know as Liberia, Nigeria, Senegal, Cameroon, Mali, and beyond. Within these regions, the people came from their own tribal and family groups, all with their own languages, traditions, customs, and religious and musical practices. For the slaver, this was of little concern. The people were captured and crammed into crowded slave ships and sent out to work upon reaching the destination. For many of those that were transported, the only language they shared in common with their fellows was English, the language of the slave masters. But on a deeper level, there was another way to communicate: the language of their varied musical traditions.

Many African languages have no word for "music" separate from other activities such as storytelling, lore-giving, and so forth. Music is integrated into life at a deep level until it *becomes* life. Even when life is uprooted, music travels with it. Music can communicate when words fail, and even when people lack a common language, they can still join together to share their inner world through playing and sharing music. By these means, the various musical traditions of the African continent were not only brought together in America but provided those who brought it with a unique means of telling their story, a means which had not previously existed in America, and which, with its non-Western tonalities and intricate rhythms, was something quite different to the music already existing in America, whether in Western classical and folk traditions or the music played by America's own First Nations peoples. The difficulty in separating music from other elements of culture is particularly challenging when we look at religious and spiritual traditions, with music forming a core part of spiritual practice in many cultures and practices ranging from *voudon* chants to the Nyabinghi drumming of Jamaica and the sung services and hymns of the Christian traditions.

The United States abolished the trans-Atlantic slave trade in 1808 when the Act Prohibiting Importation of Slaves, approved by Congress on March 2 of the previous year, took effect. Despite the ban on the trade, this was not the end of slavery. Existing slaves remained the property of their owners, and the slave trade continued illegally. Slavery continued until the Emancipation Proclamation of 1863. The last known slave ship to make landfall on the continental United States was the *Clotilda*, which bought a ship of captives from the west coast of Africa to Alabama in 1860 and was burned by its captain in an attempt to hide the evidence.

With the end of slavery, the demand for agricultural labor continued, along with a continued unwillingness to pay a fair wage in return for this labor. Sharecropping served as a replacement on many large farms and plantations. Under the sharecropping system, the laborer was ostensibly a free agent or contractor, granted a patch of land and rudimentary accommodation, which they were free to farm on behalf of the plantation owner. Basic needs and farming supplies could be purchased at a company store, often on credit against the proceeds of future crops. While some plantation owners used this system fairly to create a system agreeable to both parties, the system could be easily, and more often than not was, manipulated to ensure that the payment for the crops produced was less than the amount owed for purchases during the previous year, and so the hapless farmers found themselves in an endless cycle of debt. While these supposedly may not have been under the yoke of slavery, they were left without the financial means to leave and seek better circumstances elsewhere. In some of the largest plantations, payment was made in the form of custom-minted coins only redeemable at the plantation's store, preventing sharecroppers from saving what they could before hitting the road to try their luck elsewhere.

It has been suggested that the first blues song was sung before the invention of the phonograph, in the fields and towns, honky-tonks and juke joints. However, the recordings we do have of singers performing songs from a pre-blues era often bear only the barest resemblance to the music we know as the blues, lacking the distinct harmonic structure and form of the blues, although we can hear traces of the triplet-based syncopation and microtonal melodies that helped form later blues. Early field hollers often employed a call and response format that echoes the AAB structure of a typical twelve-bar blues.

The first African American musical form to impact the wider culture was the minstrel show. The origins of the minstrel show can be traced to the early nineteenth century as adaptations and reworkings of what was presented as traditional plantation or work songs were performed on stage, often by white performers wearing blackface. The minstrel show represented a merging of show business traditions, a variety show where popular song met opera, acrobatics, and clowning, as well as traditions of genuine African American origin such as the cakewalk.

While it is clear that minstrel shows intended to find humor in ridicule, they also provided a means for African American styles to step outside of their traditional settings and work their way into the wider culture. Minstrelsy also became a means for Black performers to showcase their genuine traditions, although, ironically, they too were expected to wear the "blackface" style makeup in order to give the crowd the kind of show they expected. These performers also experienced the paradox later experienced by blues performers who performed for white audiences in the twentieth century. While they were hailed as celebrities and applauded onstage and off-stage, they were still subject to the prejudices and restrictions of the time. Soon, popular song and dance traditions began to integrate styles adapted for the minstrel show. Many of these songs survive today, although it is doubtful that many schoolchildren are taught the song's origins when learning "Camptown Races" in second-grade music class.

Examples of the folk traditions that evolved into the blues can be heard in the recordings of the "songsters," musicians of the blues age who often performed older songs from the pre-blues tradition. While these musicians often included blues in their repertoire, the recordings of musicians such as Papa Charlie Jackson, Henry Thomas, Mississippi John Hurt, and Mance Lipscomb contain older tunes such as "Stagger Lee" and "Fishin' Blues," which have clear origins in earlier folk traditions. While traces of the blues proper can be heard, particularly in the use of so-called "blue notes," in structure and form, these songs are clearly distinct from the blues itself.

Ragtime music had its origins in the late nineteenth century, combining popular musical forms of the day with the syncopation and polyrhythms of African music to create a style of popular music played in "ragged time." The music is said to have grown out of the styles played by the piano "professors" in the saloons and brothels that grew up alongside the riverboat trade. Scott Joplin was the king of ragtime, and many of his tunes, such as "The Entertainer" (1902), best known these days from the soundtrack to the 1973 film *The Sting*, retain their popularity today.

Jazz also grew from the blending of Western musical styles with African- and Caribbean-style rhythms. The birthplace of jazz is commonly held to be New Orleans. In the nineteenth century, African Americans traditionally gathered in Congo Square, just over Rampart Street from the French Quarter in the area now known as Louis Armstrong Park, to dance, play music, and engage in spiritual practices, including voodoo ceremony. At the same time, musicians in the red-light district known as Storyville combined these rhythms with popular music of the day, including ragtime and the music of the marching bands, which were a common sight in New Orleans. Jazz became defined by its strong sense of syncopation and an emphasis on improvisation, where the expectation was for musicians to vary and extend the melody of the song they were playing. Jazz quickly became one of the most popular forms of music in America.

The relationship between jazz and blues presents us with a "chicken and egg" scenario. While it is easy to view blues as the simpler form out of which jazz grew, early forms of jazz appear to predate the blues. While jazz and blues both share a common origin, growing out of the African diaspora at roughly the same time and each influencing the other, it is hard to draw a direct line from one to the other. In the early days, the two kinds of music commonly crossed over with one another, with jazz giants such as Louis Armstrong appearing on records by blues singers and instrumentalists such as guitarist Lonnie Johnson (1899-1970), proving to be equally influential on both genres.

New Orleans native Lonnie Johnson achieved his first success in the blues world, recording sides such as "Mr. Johnson's Blues" for the Okeh label, but soon crossed over into jazz, recording with Louis Armstrong's Hot Five and Duke Ellington. Robert Johnson was such a fan of Lonnie's quick, nimble single-note work that he would claim to be related to Lonnie. Robert was not the only significant musician to have been influenced by Lonnie, who was a major inspiration on both Charlie Christian and T-Bone Walker. In his memoir *Chronicles Vol 1*, Bob Dylan cited Lonnie as a major influence on his guitar style and approach to improvisation.

While the period from the 1920s to the early '30s is commonly known as "The Jazz Age," it was the music of Hawaii that proved to be the dominant commercial force and was a major influence on popular music of the era, including the blues. The native music of Hawaii was traditionally sung with percussion accompaniment. After formal contact with Europe, the songs and melodies were soon adapted to be performed on the instruments bought by the settlers and sailors who came to the islands. The ukulele, for example, evolved from the small travel guitars carried by Portuguese sailors. In the late nineteenth century, Hawaiian musicians developed a technique of de-tuning, or slackening, the strings on the full-sized Spanish guitar to alternate tunings that better suited the traditional Hawaiian melodies. The techniques of this "slack key" guitar style, including hammer-ons, pull-offs, and vibrato, are also part of the blues guitarists' stock-in-trade. Hawaiian guitar developed even further when, in the 1890s, the lap steel technique was developed, supposedly by the young guitarist Joseph Kekuku (1874-1932), who was inspired to fret his guitar with a bolt he found discarded on the ground.

In the early twentieth century, Hawaiian musicians toured the continental United States, bringing their slack key and lap steel techniques with them. African American musicians who encountered this music would have found some of it familiar. Instruments played with the slide can be found in many African traditions, and the one-string diddley bow certainly pre-dates the Hawaiian music craze, while the open tunings of the slack key guitar were similar to the tunings used on the banjo and its African predecessors. By 1915, Hawaiian music was the best-selling music in America, both on record and in print. So that fans of the music could play the sheet music they bought, the instruments needed—including guitars modified for slide playing—became readily available in-store and via mail order through channels such as the Sears catalogue. A strong case can certainly be made that the sounds of Hawaiian music can be heard in the blues that followed, but more significantly, the Hawaiian music craze made the tools needed to play the blues cheaper and more readily available.

By the early 20th century, African American musicians across the United States were playing styles of music that could be identified as the blues. W.C. Handy (1973-1958), the self-described "father of the blues," describes in his autobiography how he encountered these styles while leading his popular band through the South:

> The band, which I found in Clarksdale, and the nine-man orchestra which grew out of it, did yeoman duty in the Delta. We played for affairs of every description. I came to know by heart every foot of the Delta, even from Clarksdale to Lambert on the Dog and Yazoo City. I could call every stop, water tower and pig path on the Peavine with my eyes closed. It all became a familiar, monotonous round. Then one night in Tutwiler, as I nodded in the railroad station while waiting for a train that had been delayed nine hours, life suddenly took me by the shoulder and wakened me with a start.
>
> A lean, loose-jointed Negro had commenced plunking a guitar beside me while I slept. His clothes were rags, his feet peeped out of his shoes. As he played, he pressed a knife on the strings of the guitar in a manner popularized by Hawaiian guitarists who use steel bars. The effect was unforgettable. His song, too, struck me instantly. 'Goin' where the Southern cross' the Dog.' The singer repeated the line three times, accompanying himself on the guitar with the weirdest music I had ever

heard.[1]

Later on, he describes performing at a dance in Mississippi when one of the local performers requested to take the stage while the band was on break and playing some local blues. Handy relishes describing the rain of dimes, quarters, and dollars that fell on the stage in appreciation of the music being played. It was this, perhaps more than any love of the music, that convinced Handy that it was worth taking his inspiration from this local style.

It is worth noting that Handy's band was based in Clarksdale, today the home of the famous Crossroads monument and a city that has played a significant role as a hub of the blues throughout the music's history. Many of the most important blues musicians, such as Muddy Waters, John Lee Hooker, and Ike Turner, were born or raised in the city and surrounding area. Clarksdale's location in the Delta also made it an important stopping-off point for anyone traveling from further South to Memphis and the North.

Handy wrote his first blues number, "Memphis Blues," in 1909. Based on a campaign song used by Tennessee politician Edward Crump, the song combines twelve-bar and longer sixteen-bar blues forms with a ragtime rhythm popular at the time. Handy published the sheet music for "Memphis Blues" in September 1912, but the song would not achieve much success until the first recordings of the tune were released two years later. Handy returned to the blues form again in the same year with "St. Louis Blues," a song that would become one of his biggest successes. While Handy's blues were the first songs using the blues form that achieved widespread popularity, they were not the first blues songs published. Earlier examples of published sheet music using the blues form include Anthony Maggio's "I Got the Blues" in 1908 and Hart Wand's "Dallas Blues" in 1912.

With the popularity of "Memphis Blues" and its follow-ups, the blues became a genuine craze, although not one often heard on record. Despite recordings of Handy's tunes increasing their exposure, the big money in music at the time was in sheet music. Record players were less common than instruments, and if people wanted to hear a favorite song, they would purchase the sheet music and perform it for themselves. The first blues recording was not released until August 10, 1920, when the Okeh label issued Mamie Smith's performance of Perry Bradford's "Crazy Blues."

The recording was a genuine smash, selling over 75,000 copies in its first month of release and ushering in the golden age of classic female blues. Record buyers rushed for new releases by the likes of Bessie Smith, Ma Rainey, Victoria Spivey, and Sippie Wallace. Record sales were driven by newer, more affordable record players, allowing music fans to hear and purchase music they may never have heard performed live, and by the fact that this was music by black performers aimed at a black market. The records, which sold in the hundreds of thousands, spoke directly to their listeners. Bessie Smith sang of experiences of racism, of poverty, of gambling, and also of freedom, independence, and free sexuality. Ma Rainey sang openly of lesbianism and bisexuality. We can see here how the blues gained its reputation as the Devil's music. No good churchgoer would openly admit to listening to such tunes, no matter what the evidence of their record collection said.

The first commercial release by a solo male performer came out in 1924 with Papa Charlie Jackson's "Airy Man Blues." Accompanying himself on the six-string "banjitar," Jackson specialized in humorous, bawdy songs. His records sold well; however, his legacy was eclipsed by Texan bluesman Blind Lemon Jefferson, who was the first genuine star of what we would consider the country blues, playing stripped-back tunes that even at the time were advertised as rural and old fashioned. Urban record buyers flocked to purchase these records, which reminded them of music they heard "back home." Songs such as "Matchbox Blues" and "See That My Grave Is Kept Clean" became standards whose popularity persists today. Sadly, Jefferson's success would be short-lived. He passed away in 1929, just three years after the release of his first blues record. Rumors persist that, like Robert Johnson,

Jefferson was poisoned by a lover's jealous partner. Jefferson's fame can be heard in the Reverend Emmett Dickinson's recorded sermon "Death of Blind Lemon," in which the preacher tells us that Lemon's life was "in many respects like that of our Lord Jesus Christ. Like him, until the age of 30 he was unknown … in a short space of a little over three years his name and works were known in every home."

While Blind Lemon Jefferson played in a rural Texas style, it was Charlie Patton (spelled "Charley" on his record labels) who proved that Mississippi Delta blues could be a commercial force. He was born in 1891 and raised on the Dockery Plantation in Sunflower County, Mississippi, just outside of Ruleville. Singing with a distinct, gravel-tinged voice, Patton played the guitar in a heavily rhythmic style, mixing his right- and left-hand rhythms with the stomping of his feet to create complex polyrhythms strongly reminiscent of the distinct 3 over 4 rhythms of West Africa. Patton was a showman, known for spinning and juggling his guitar, anticipating later performers like T-Bone Walker, Jimi Hendrix, and Stevie Ray Vaughan by playing his instrument behind his head or between his knees. After auditioning for talent scout and record-label fixer H.C. Spier (who would later audition Johnson), Patton recorded "Pony Blues," which was released on the Paramount label in 1929. The song was a success and remains a standard among Delta musicians to this day. Patton's success was such that his third record, "Screamin' and Hollerin' the Blues," could be released under the pseudonym "The Masked Marvel" and included a competition entry slip encouraging listeners to guess which Paramount artist was singing the tune, with a selection of Paramount releases offered as a prize.

Son House was another major artist of the early Delta blues. Most likely born in 1902, House had spent time as a preacher and spiritual singer before turning to the blues in his mid-20s. This pull between the sacred and the secular helps create a unique tension in House's music, as the driving, almost sexual rhythms of his slashing slide guitar combine with his voice that hits home like a sermon; at times, he appears to be on the verge of speaking in tongues. This tension can be heard in songs such as "Preachin' the Blues," later adapted by Johnson as "Preachin' Blues (Up Jumped the Devil)," and itself derived from a Bessie Smith song of the same name, which House recorded for Paramount in 1929. House's commercial releases were unsuccessful, but he remained a popular local performer and recorded again in 1941 for the Library of Congress before giving up on blues, moving to New York, and working odd jobs before his rediscovery by blues enthusiasts in the early 1960s led to a second career on the festival and coffee house circuit. House retired from music again in 1974, moving to Detroit, Michigan, where he passed away in 1988, one of the last living links to the earliest days of the blues. The combination of timing and longevity, mixed with his doubtless talent and the quality of his performances, is what makes House a central figure in the history of the blues. He played with both Charley Patton and the legendary Willie Brown as name-checked in Johnson's "Crossroad Blues." After his rediscovery, he played with and influenced latter-day disciples such as Rory Block, Bonnie Raitt, and Canned Heat's Al "Blind Owl" Wilson, the latter of whom not only recorded with House but was also given the unenviable task of helping House to relearn how to play in his former style. In between, House was also influential on major figures such as Howlin' Wolf and Muddy Waters, as well as Robert Johnson.

Willie Brown was born on August 6, 1900, in Clarksdale, Mississippi. He is known to have recorded six sides for the Paramount label, of which only two, "M & O Blues" and "Future Blues," are known to have survived. Willie's style typifies the Delta blues style, with strong, deep rhythms. Brown mostly worked as an accompanist, playing second guitar behind Son House and Charley Patton, among others. Much of Robert Johnson's guitar technique can be understood as an attempt to imitate the rhythmic and melodic intricacies of this two-guitar style, echoes of which can also be heard in the guitar interplay between Muddy Waters and Jimmy Rogers in their '50s recordings for Chicago's Chess label. Despite finding little success as a recording artist, Willie Brown remained a popular local live performer up until his death in 1952.

A MEETING AT THE CROSSROADS: ROBERT JOHNSON AND THE DEVIL

Born in Bentonia, Mississippi, Skip James (1901-1969) played in a unique, modal, minor-key style that had been taught to him by fellow Bentonia musician Henry Stuckey, based on tuning the guitar to an open E minor chord. Stuckey had learned this tuning from Bahamian soldiers he had met while serving in the First World War, who used the tuning to play their own deeply African-rooted folk and popular songs. James recorded for the Paramount label in 1921, and 18 sides were released. While they did not sell in huge numbers, his influence can be heard in Johnson's "32-20 Blues," based on James's piano-based "22-20 Blues" and "Hell Hound on My Trail," which imitates the distinct sound of songs such as "Devil Got My Woman" and "Hard Time Killing Floor Blues." James was rediscovered in 1964 and bought onto the festival and coffee shop circuit, recording a number of well-received albums. Royalties from supergroup Cream's cover of "I'm So Glad" (included on both the band's debut *Fresh Cream* and farewell album *Goodbye*) paid for his funeral expenses.

Lizzie Douglas (1897-1973), also known by her recording name Memphis Minnie, is best known today for her 1929 song "When the Levee Breaks," which described the experiences of the Mississippi floods of 1927, and was famously covered by Led Zeppelin on their fourth, untitled album. This song was recorded with Kansas Joe McCoy, the second of her three husbands. Tough and straight-shooting, she could present a ladylike figure on stage but was able to cut heads with her instrument or defend herself with a razor as the situation demanded. Her 1941 song "Me and My Chauffeur" has become a standard, attracting answer songs and cover versions from artists ranging from Lightnin' Hopkins to Jefferson Airplane. She traveled in the same circles as Johnson and was certainly known to Johnson's traveling and musical partner Johnny Shines. Annye C. Anderson describes a party and jam session at which both Minnie and Johnson were present, and songs like "Bumble Bee" may have been an influence on Johnson's playing. Her music continues to be an inspiration to blues artists today.

Thanks in part to the success of Robert Johnson, the image of a lone singer and his guitar is central to the Delta blues in the popular imagination, yet arguably the most popular Delta act of the 1930s was the fiddle-led combo the Mississippi Sheiks. Based around members of the Chatmon family, the Sheiks had a large, rotating lineup that reportedly allowed them to field two different lineups of the band on the same night when double-booked. The enduring legacy of the Mississippi Sheiks lives on today through their signature tune, the eight-bar blues "Sittin' on Top of the World," which continues to be a standard at blues concerts and jam sessions the world over. Johnson was clearly familiar with the song and used it as the melodic template for "Come on in My Kitchen." Armenter Chatmon, a member of their performing band who was featured on a number of the Sheiks' recordings, also found success recording under the name Bo Carter, releasing over 100 sides of sexually suggestive tunes with titles like "Banana in Your Fruit Basket" and "Please Warm My Wiener."

"Sittin' on Top of the World" shares some melodic similarities with the earlier hit "How Long, How Long Blues," recorded in 1928 by the piano and guitar duo Leroy Carr (1905-1935) and Scrapper Blackwell (1903-1962). Carr and Blackwell were among the biggest male recording artists of their era, combining Carr's slow-rocking, piano-crooning vocal style, later an influence on the likes of Charles Brown and Ray Charles, with Blackwell's sophisticated single-string lines on guitar.

Blues was as popular in the northern states as it was in the South. This was partly due to the mass migration of African Americans to the northern cities in search of work. Although largely forgotten today except by the aficionado, the brothers Aaron "Pinetop" and Marion Sparks, recording as the Sparks Brothers, provide one example of this. Although raised in Tupelo, Mississippi, the two brothers found a home in St. Louis, where they made a reputation for themselves playing a mix of Delta and up-tempo jump blues. While their recorded output was small, made in just a few short years between 1932 and 1935, it proved influential, including standards such as "Every Day I Have the Blues" and "61 Highway Blues," as well as the lesser-known number, "I

Believe I'll Make a Change," which provided the template for Johnson's "I Believe I'll Dust My Broom."

Pre-war blues often featured songs about the Devil, who was often depicted as a Trickster or joker, a figure who could stand outside of and poke fun at societal norms. One of the earliest of these Devil songs is Clara Smith's 1924 tune "Done Sold My Soul to the Devil," in which she uses the symbol of a deal with The Devil to represent her role as a blues performer and her separation from polite society.

Of the male blues singers, Peatie Wheatstraw (1902-1939) was the one with the strongest association with the Devil. Known as the "High Sheriff of Hell" and "The Devil's Son-In-Law," Wheatstraw sang darkly humorous songs that occasionally touched on diabolical themes. Wheatstraw's impact was such that he eventually ended up entering African American folklore as an archetypal "bad man" figure akin to Stagger Lee and Dolemite, was the subject of toasts and street rhymes, and was even depicted in Blaxploitation cinema by Rudy Ray Moore, where he recasts the Peatie from folklore as a street hustler who competes with the Devil for the ownership of a magical "pimp cane."

Tommy Johnson (1896-1956) is another name that often comes up when discussing the blues and the Devil. An associate of Charley Patton and Willie Brown, Tommy sang songs in the Delta style that were often darkly realistic. In 1928's "Canned Heat Blues" (which gave its name to the '60s blues revival band), Johnson sings of drinking strained Sterno cooking fuel as a substitute for alcohol. Tommy was not related to Robert and no record exists of any direct meeting between the two, although as they knew the same people and played on the same scene, the possibility cannot be dismissed. Tommy's association with Robert and the Devil comes from his brother LeDell's claim that Tommy had gained his guitar skills through a midnight crossroads deal with the Devil.

The music of Memphis was central in the history of the blues and in Robert Johnson's development as a musician. One of the most important and commercially successful of the Memphis blues subgenres was jug band music. By combining the sounds of homemade and low-cost instruments such as the jug, washboard, tea-chest bass, or kazoo with music based on the popular ragtime and jazz-based sounds, jug music created a unique fusion between uptown and down-home sounds. Bands such as Gus Cannon's Jug Stompers proved to be reliable sellers and were popular live attractions, particularly in Memphis where they could pull good money both in the clubs and playing for tips on the street. Jug music experienced its heyday on the streets of Memphis during Robert's childhood, and you can hear it echoed in the hokum-inspired "They're Red Hot" and the double-entendres of "Terraplane Blues" and "Phonograph Blues."

Hudson Woodbridge (1903-1981), better known as Tampa Red, was one of the most successful urban musicians of the pre-war era. He played slide guitar with a clear, ringing sound reminiscent of the Hawaiian steel guitarists popular at the time. His repertoire ranged from double-entendre hokum tunes such as "What Is It That Taste Like Gravy" to topical songs like "Depressions Blues" and songs that would later become standards, including "Black Angel Blues," first recorded by Lucille Bogan and made world-famous by B.B. King as "Sweet Little Angel," and "It Hurts Me Too," which became a hit for Elmore James when he recorded it for the Fire label in 1962. His influence can be heard in Johnson's clear and precise bottleneck style, standing in sharp contrast to the more percussive playing typical of the Delta.

By Johnson's time, the blues had grown into a rich and diverse genre. Far from the stereotype of a primitive music enjoyed strictly by farmers and sharecroppers, it was the music of the hip and slick and could be heard in urban bars and lounges, as well as the plantations and juke joints. Those who would prefer to see the blues purely as an ancestor of rock 'n' roll are doing the music a great disservice. This was, and still is, a continuously growing and evolving tradition. As we will see, Robert was positioned to see all diverse facets of the blues of his day, and even anticipate the electric blues still to come, as he moved from Mississippi to Memphis and beyond, and was able to combine these diverse influences with his own personal genius to create his own singular style.

[1] Handy, 1941, p 74

The Life and Times of Robert Johnson

The stabbing sounds from the guitar could almost break a window. When Johnson started singing, he seemed like a guy who could have sprung from the head of Zeus in full armor.
   - **Bob Dylan[1]**

When he first came to public attention, Robert Johnson was a man without a face or a story. Little was known about him, and what was known was based on unreliable or anecdotal sources. The original liner notes to the 1961 LP *King of the Delta Blues Singers* describe Johnson as "...little, very little more than a name on aging index cards and a few dusty master records in the files of a phonograph company that no longer exists." Since that time, the gaps have slowly been filled. It is thanks to the tireless research of a small army of researchers tracking down church records and interviewing people who knew Robert that we are now able to build up an accurate picture of his life. The discovery is still ongoing with the research of Bruce Conforth and Gayle Dean Wardlow, revealing many previously unknown details, and the first-hand accounts of Annye C. Anderson, giving us a stronger picture of Johnson as a person.

Hazlehurst is the seat of Copiah County, Mississippi, just under forty miles south of Jackson. Like many small towns in Mississippi, whatever inner-city life Hazlehurst once had has been largely transferred to the Walmart on the edge of town. Times were better back in the late nineteenth century, when it served as a major rail hub, bringing some degree of wealth to the area.

Most of that is gone now, although the *City of New Orleans* passenger train passes through most days, winding its way from New Orleans to Chicago. If you wander down to the old depot in the middle of town, you'll find a small museum dedicated to the music Mississippi has given to the world, with pride of place given to the city's most famous son, Robert Johnson.

Johnson was born in Hazlehurst on May 8, 1911, the eleventh child of Julia Majors Dodds. His father was Noah Johnson, a local farmhand. At the time, Julia was still married to another man, Charles Dodds, a local landowner and manufacturer of wicker furniture. The relationship between Julia and Charles had soured when Charles hit upon hard times and angered the wrong people. Locals told stories of Charles disguising himself in women's clothes in order to escape a lynch mob after angering the Marchettis, an influential family of white local landowners. It was after this enforced separation that Julia hooked up with Noah Johnson. Julia and her children stayed with Noah for about two years; however, the pressure of raising such a large family on a farmhand's limited income caused the relationship to become strained, and no doubt there was some resentment on Noah's part in paying for the upkeep of children fathered by another man.

Gradually, the younger children were sent to Memphis to live with their father, who in the meantime had started going by the name Charles Spencer and had taken a live-in mistress. Finally, Julia and Robert made the journey to Memphis to live in this unusual household consisting of a man, his new mistress and their children, his former wife and their children, plus Julia's child by another man. It was about this time that Robert took the name Robert Spencer, after the assumed name of the head of the household and his current father figure. A short time after this, perhaps struggling with the strain of the mixed household, perhaps caught up by her own wanderlust, Julia left the household to continue an itinerant existence in Mississippi.

Memphis, Tennessee is a city that punches above its weight in terms of cultural influence. It's never been a large city. As of 2021, the population of the city proper is still well short of a million, yet it is a city that looms large in the myths of America. It was an early center of the blues; it gave us Sun Studios, B.B. King and Elvis Presley, the soul of Stax and Hi Records, and a whole lot more. Its story is echoed in song, ranging from W.C. Handy's "Memphis Blues" to the AOR rock of "Walking in Memphis," the Afro-pop fusion of Paul Simon's *Graceland*, and the lo-fi hip-hop of Al Kapone and Gangsta Pat (himself the son of legendary Stax Records drummer Willie Hall). Memphis has always been a transport hub, both of the steamboats that piled up and down the Mississippi and the railway running across the country. The music that comes out of Memphis echoes the life and aspirations of the country as a whole, speaking bitter truths and offering the promise of escape.

It was during his time living with the Spencers in Memphis that Robert received his first in-depth exposure to the blues. Memphis was a musical hub, a place where musicians and musical forms met and new music was created. Robert's older half brother Charles would later become known as a pianist, and it is perhaps through Charles that Robert first discovered the music of W.C. Handy and other early blues composers, whose works were commonly sold as sheet music to be played in the home. Interviews with those who knew Robert all agree that his first instruments were the jaw harp and the diddley bow. Neither instrument requires much in the way of skill. You can learn to pick out a simple melody on the jaw harp in a matter of minutes. The diddley bow is more interesting. It is almost the traditional first instrument of bluesmen of the era, consisting of nothing more than a piece of wire nailed to the wall or on a plank of wood with a stick wedged underneath to act as a bridge. The musician plucks the wire and slides a smooth object such as a pipe, bottleneck, or screwdriver across to vary the pitch and to allow the player to pick out a tune or melody. With practice, the skilled diddley bow player could take advantage of the fretless nature of the instrument to imitate the sounds of the human voice and hit the microtonal pitches that are critical sounds in blues music.

Memphis would also have given Robert the opportunity to expose himself to the rich African American musical traditions that centered around Beale Street. Beale Street was not just a center of blues but all elements of black American culture, including the rhyming street talk and "toasts," telling stories of semi-mythical figures such as the notorious Stagger Lee (or Stack O'Lee, depending on which version you prefer). Memphis and the Beale Street district were also centers of hoodoo culture. Hoodoo items such as hot foot powder and mojo hands were available for purchase at stores such as A. Schwab's Dry Goods (opened in 1876 and still going, with the motto "If you can't find it at Schwab's, you're better off without it") and any number of spiritual doctors and healers who practiced in the area.

Exposure to some practices was not unique to Robert's experience, but it is safe to assume that Robert's awareness of these spiritual practices was on par with any other young African American growing up in the area at the time. While earlier researchers such as Julio Finn have suggested that the real, and sometimes perceived, reference to magical practices in Johnson's songs are evidence that Robert was a formal initiate in the voodoo and hoodoo traditions; what references to voodoo we do find in Johnson's lyrics, such as the mention of a "nation sack" in *Come On In My Kitchen*, are of a type familiar enough to any African American of the time, particularly one who had spent some time wandering up and down Beale Street Or was aware of the spiritual doctors and advisors common in the Delta. Even at his young age, Robert would have been aware of such things in the same way that a modern child might be aware of their mother consulting her horoscope.

After four years in Memphis, Robert was sent back to Mississippi to live again with his mother, who had taken up with a sharecropper named Dusty Willis and moved to the Abbay & Leatherman Plantation, near Robinsville. By all accounts, Robert and Dusty didn't get along, and it is about this time that Robert started going by his birth father's family name, insisting on being called Robert Johnson. We see here the beginnings of a pattern that Robert would continue in later life, changing his name and identity as suited his mood and circumstances; in this case, deliberately choosing the name of his birth father to send a message regarding his identity to both his mother and her current partner.

At this time, Robert was also enrolled in formal schooling. Based on the stories told by those who knew and played with him, such as fellow blues men Honeyboy Edwards and Robert Lockwood Jr., we know Robert was able to read and write. Formal schooling, however, was held back by troubles with his eyesight, possibly caused by a cataract in his left eye. This cataract can be clearly seen in one of three known photographs of Johnson, the so-called "photo booth" picture, where Johnson stares menacingly at the camera, a cigarette dangling from his mouth, attempting to invoke the bad-man spirit of Stagger Lee and the bluesmen of Memphis and the Delta. As with many children before and since, this minor disability prevented Johnson from achieving his full potential. Soon enough, however, he was able to find other ways to spend his time, ways that might provide a better living than a mere sharecropper could hope for.

Robert started playing the blues in earnest when he was about fifteen. Beginning with the harmonica, an instrument that was readily available and affordable on a farmhand's salary, he also started getting more serious about stringed instruments, moving from the diddley bow up to a cheap, homemade contraption fashioned out of a cigar box and baling twine, and from there to a second-hand guitar that was missing two strings. This musical interest placed further strain on Robert's relationship with Willis, who saw no value in a skill that could not be used to farm the land. Robert seemed to pay this no mind and could be found playing the guitar out in the field in the middle of the working day. His repertoire was varied but consisted largely of folk and popular tunes. Where he did play blues songs, he would imitate the urban styles he had heard in Memphis such as the music of W.C. Handy, and the hokum sounds of jug band music.

The lure of Memphis was still strong, and Robert took to regularly hitchhiking his way to and from the city, no doubt partly to visit an environment where he had once known stronger family bonds, but also to encounter the blues and to explore the bars, urban jukes, and "buckets o' blood" where the music could be found. After he turned 16, Robert was able to purchase a second-hand T-Model Ford, and this served to make Memphis even more accessible. By visiting Memphis, Robert was able to keep abreast of the latest trends in black culture. While people who stayed in rural Mississippi might stick to clothes and musical styles that were years, perhaps even decades, out of vogue, a man with a car was able to keep up with the latest trends, the latest cuts in suits, and the hippest, freshest music. Annye C. Anderson tells us that Robert was a regular cinemagoer with a particular enthusiasm for Westerns, including the "Singing Cowboy" Gene Autry. Coin-operated "VoiceOGraph" recording booths, where for the cost of a few coins a brief recording could be made and pressed onto a 78 rpm record, were common. We can suppose that Robert, keen to work on his style, may have recorded himself in one of these booths. Sadly, any trace of this has now been lost.

On February 17, 1929, at the age of seventeen, Johnson married fourteen-year-old Virginia Travis. On the marriage certificate, he signs himself as Robert Johnson, a sign that he was now assured of his identity and considered himself independent from both the Spencers and his mother's partner. Travis was pregnant with Robert's child and Robert appeared to, at least temporarily, turn his back on his musical ambitions and dedicate himself to becoming a father and a provider. He still traveled from time to time and continued to perform when the opportunity arose, but his focus was now on his family.

Robert and Virginia made a home for themselves east of Robinsville on the Kline plantation, sharing their lodgings with Virginia's half sister Bessie and her husband. However, any hopes of a happy and perhaps even settled family life were cruelly swept away when Virginia died during childbirth, along with her child, in April of the same year. According to most accounts, Robert was not present at the time of the deaths. He was away traveling for either work or music, if not both, and returned home expecting to find a wife and newborn child, only to discover that fate had taken them away.

We can only speculate on the impact this had on Johnson and his ambitions. It is easy to draw the conclusion that this was the breaking point that drove Robert toward the life of a blues musician. While Travis's passing certainly appears to have caused Johnson to abandon any hope he may have had of settling down and living a life as a dedicated family man and laborer, there is little to no evidence that he was ever fully committed to the settled life. We can safely speculate that living as he was with his now-late wife's family members, Robert would have found himself an unwelcome or at least uncomfortable presence in the household. In that case, he may have taken the life of an itinerant musician partly through necessity rather than choice, suddenly finding that not only had his family been taken from him but with it his place to live, along with the means to earn a livelihood on the plantation. He may have chosen how to play his hand, but he did not choose the cards he was dealt.

What we do know is that by 1930, the great Delta blues singer Son House was encountering Robert as a regular figure at juke joints and house parties. According to House's account, the young Robert was keen to play guitar and take part in the rowdy juke joint sessions, but his enthusiasm was not matched by his skill. At the time, House was traveling with Willie Brown, and the two worked in partnership, entertaining the crowds. The young, enthusiastic Robert was keen to keep the party jumping when House and Brown took a break to gamble or drink, but if House is to be believed, he was more likely to clear the room than keep the party going.

House gives the following account of Robert's playing in a 1965 interview with Richard Lester for 'Sing Out' magazine,

> *We'd all play for the Saturday night balls, and there'd be this little boy standing around. That was Robert Johnson. And when we'd get a break and want to rest some, we'd set the guitars up in the corner and go out in the cool. Robert would watch and see which way we'd gone, and he would pick one of them up. And such another racket you never heard! It'd make*

> the people mad, you know. They'd come out and say, 'Why don't y'all go in there and get that guitar away from that boy! He's running people crazy with it.'

In a separate interview from the same year, this time with John Fahey, we hear the same story told again,

> So Robert, he would be standing around and he would listen too, and he got the idea that he'd like to play. So he started out from that and everywhere that he'd get to hear us playing for a Saturday night ball, he would come up and be there...So when we'd get a rest period or something, we'd set the guitars up and go out - and it would be hot in the summertime, so we'd go out and get in the cool, cool off some. While we're out, Robert, he'd get the guitar and go to bamming with it, you know? Just keeping noise, and the people didn't like that. They'd come and tell us, 'Why don't you or Willie go in there and stop that boy? He's driving everybody nuts...' But as quick as we're out there again, and get to laughing and talking and drinking, here, we'd hear the guitar going again, making all kinds of tunes, 'Bloo Wah, Boom Wah.' A dog wouldn't want to hear it.

Like many a keen amateur, Johnson's ambition exceeded his ability. He had adopted the styles and stance of the juke joint musician, hanging out in the right places and getting to know the right people, but he was missing the crucial ingredient. The talking-the-talk was all there, but he was seriously lacking in the walking-the-walk department. While Robert was at this stage certainly no raw beginner, it is likely that the music he played was not the music his audience wanted to hear.

Whatever his experience, Robert's earlier repertoire was not of the Delta blues style he was later known for. Perhaps it was unfair of House to say that Robert was not yet a skilled musician, but more accurate to say that he was not skilled at playing the style of music that the juke joint audiences wanted to hear. His trips to Memphis may have kept him abreast of the latest trends, but the Memphis style tended to the more slick and urbane, where the blues mixed with the sounds of the jazz age and even the homegrown genre of jug band music, itself feeding off the syncopated styles of New Orleans jazz. This was a very different thing from the driving, deeply rhythmic sounds that the juke joint and house party crowds in the Delta wanted to hear while they danced, caroused, and gambled.

After playing around on the scene for a while, filling in when established acts took a break, playing at the jukes and parties when he was able and slowly learning his trade, Robert just up and disappeared. Some accounts say he went wandering off to Hazlehurst to find his birth father, while others suggest that after his hard experiences at a young age, Robert needed to go wandering, get out of town and start walking. Johnny Shines and Honeyboy Edwards both described how, when they knew him, Robert was a wanderer, never keen to stay in one place for too long, and it is likely this wanderlust that struck him now. The call came, and he was booked and bound to go.

The timespan of Robert's absence is difficult to determine. Going by House's account, it was quite short, only about three months, but estimates range up to a year or even longer. Whatever the case was, on his return, Johnson's playing had undergone a transformation, one considered remarkable given the length of time he had been away. Returning again to Son House's account, this time describing his next encounter with Robert:

Me and Willie (Brown), we was playing out at a little place called Banks, Mississippi. I looked and I saw somebody squeezing in the front door, and I seed it was Robert. I said 'Bill, Bill.' He said, Huh.' I said, 'Look who's coming in the door, got a guitar on his back.' He said, 'Yeah, no kidding.' He said, 'Oh, that's little Robert.' I said, 'Yeah, that's him.' I said, 'Don't say nothing.' And he wiggled his way through the crowd, until he got over to where we was. I said, 'Boy, now where you going with that thing? T'annoy somebody else to death again?' He said, 'I'll tell you what, too.' He said, 'This your rest time?' I said, 'Well, we can make it our rest time. What you want to do, annoy the folks?' He said, 'No, just let me — give me a try.' So I said, 'All right, and you better do something with it, too,' and I winked my eye at Willie. So he sat down there and finally got started. And man! He was so good! When he finished, all our mouths were standing open."

In another interview, with Pete Welding for *Sing Out!* Magazine in 1966, when pressed by the interviewer about the sudden transformation, House explained "He must have sold his soul to the Devil in exchange for learning to play like that."

Clearly, something had happened during this time away. Popular accounts indicate that this was the time when Robert made his fateful pact, and it has even been suggested that during this period he was initiated into a voodoo cult. All this lies in the realm of speculation as there is precious little evidence for such theories other than an imaginative interpretation of Robert's songs and hunches based on snatches of knowledge regarding folk-magical practices. What we do know is that it was during this period that Johnson hooked up with his early mentor Ike Zimmerman (spelled "Zinneman" in some sources), who made his home in Hazlehurst, near Robert's birthplace. Born in Grady, Alabama in 1898, Ike was already an experienced musician and seemed to take eagerly to the role of teacher and mentor. Robert may have been lured back to Hazlehurst in search of his birth father. While there is no record of Johnson encountering Noah Johnson during this time, we can make a strong case that in Zimmerman, he found something of a surrogate father figure. According to the testimony of Zimmerman's family, Ike and Robert first met in the juke joints, where Ike would play guitar and chase women, but before long, Robert moved into the Zimmerman household, where he lived with the family for an extended period of at least six or seven months.

It is during this period that we get our first definite whiff of the supernatural in Johnson's biography. Ike was a man of a number of eccentricities, not the least of which was his preferred time and place for giving Robert guitar lessons: at midnight in the graveyard across the road from the family home. According to Zimmerman's family, this is where the term crossroads comes from:

> There weren't no crossroads. They went 'cross the road. 'Cause you gotta go across (the) road and go to that cemetery. They went over there and sat on the tombstones. [2]

Whatever the practical reasons for choosing to play in such a unique location, Zimmerman was also aware of the supernatural implications of his choice of venue. His daughter said:

> He said (he'd go to the cemetery) 'cause he could play better 'cause it was still ... real quiet. Real quiet. But he'd come back and tell them he played for the, the haints (ghosts). He said he'd been there playing for the haints. They'd make a big laugh out of it. They sure would...[3]

She also assured us of how seriously Ike took his role as mentor:

> I think when he was carrying Robert up there (to the graveyard), it was so Robert could really concentrate on his guitar ... He was determined not to let him fail.[4]

As a guitar player, Ike played the Delta style of mixing fingerpicking with bottleneck slide, a style that can be clearly heard in Robert's recordings. He was also adept at the tricks of the guitar showman's trade, "juggling," spinning and throwing the guitar and playing behind his head. While some musicians may have frowned on such techniques (Son House was never impressed by what he termed Charley Patton's "clowning"), when you're being paid in tips and corn liquor, being able to put on a show can be the difference between an unsuccessful night and a full tip jar. Having all eyes in the room on you can have other benefits as well. Zimmerman was known as a womanizer and used his prowess on the guitar to chase women. This is certainly a lesson that Robert took to heart. Muddy Waters gives us a description of the informal Delta parties of the kind the pair would play at. "Saturday night is your big night. Everybody used to fry up fish and have one hell of a time ... And they really liked the low-down blues."

In later life, Zimmerman would turn back on the blues and take to preaching before dying of a heart attack in 1967. At this point in his life, however, he was committed to not just playing the blues but, at least in the case of his young protégé, to passing on what he knew. Ike and Robert would play not just the jukes but lumber and work camps, travelling by foot between gigs and often being away from home for extended periods. Finally, when Robert was ready, he was sent out to perform on his own, and he moved out of the Zimmerman family home. While there are reports that Zimmerman and Johnson teamed up to play whenever Johnson visited the area during his years as a walking musician, it is not known if Ike was ever aware of Robert's later recording career, although he certainly lived long enough to have potentially encountered Robert's records in reissue or heard Elmore James and others recording Johnson's tunes.

The mentor-student relationship between Ike and Robert is one that raises many questions. We do not know why Ike took such a shine to Robert to the extent that he let him become practically part of the family. Such mentor and student relationships are far from unknown in the blues—Muddy Waters practically made a habit of it—but this is unusual partially because Zimmerman is himself such an obscure figure. As far as is known, he made no recordings and didn't travel widely. Yet he clearly had enough of a local reputation to be seen as an authority and a teacher. Certainly, what he had to teach must have been worthwhile in order to motivate Robert, always one with itchy feet and an urge to travel, to stay in one place for so long. Equally unusual is the abrupt end of the relationship. Once Robert learned what he needed to know, the relationship ended, and he went out to prove his skills in the world.

The relationship is reminiscent of the systems of master and apprentice employed by the medieval craft guilds that later evolved into initiatory organizations such as the Freemasons. Here, the apprentice would learn at his master's side, less through direct instruction and more by observation and imitation. Once his master has assessed his skills, the former apprentice is then sent on his way as a journeyman to find work and prove himself without further instruction, until such time as his work reaches the level of a master and he can take on an apprentice of his own. I am not, of course, proposing a system of formal degrees and initiation in learning to play the blues; however, the threefold structure of student, journeyman, and master seems to hold. John Lee Hooker consistently maintained that he learned his style in a similar manner from his stepfather, Will Moore. It is reflected in Son House's relationship with Charley Patton and then in Muddy Waters's learning his own style by watching House play, in Waters's journey from the plantation to Chicago, and in his subsequent mentorship of Junior Wells and Buddy Guy, among others.

What we do know is that it was after this period that Robert had come into being as a bluesman and took up his career as a walking musician in earnest. Leaving the Hazlehurst area, he began rambling, going from town to town, serving as a journeyman musician. He seemed to have no particular goal: Traveling was an end in itself, rather than a means. He traveled far—rumors persist that he visited Chicago, New York, and even Canada; however, these are impossible to verify. His traveling and performing partner, Johnny Shines, who took up with Johnson in 1933 when he himself was just seventeen, gives an idea of how Robert was quick to find a change of scene.

> *Robert liked to travel. You could wake up any time of night and say, 'Let's go,' and he was ready. He never asked you where or why or anything. He would get up and get dressed and get ready to go. And I often say, I guess him and I were the first hippies because we didn't care when, where, or how. If we wanted to go someplace, we went. We didn't care how we went. We'd ride, walk. If you asked us where we were going, we didn't*

know. Just anywhere.

Robert may have mastered the Delta blues, but he was always ready to adapt his style as needed. His repertoire extended far beyond the blues, and he was happy to perform country, popular tunes, or even a polka if that was what it took to earn a few coins. Johnson had a good ear and was able to play back a song after hearing it only once. This was a valuable skill on the road when tastes in music could change between one town and the next. The savvy musician needed to be adaptable and ready to play what the local market demanded if he wanted to keep his belly and his purse full.

Shines also tells us how Robert managed to find the comforts of home while on the road.

> *Women were like motel or hotel rooms. Even if he used them repeatedly, he left them where he found them. He preferred older women in their 30s over the younger ones because the older ones would pay his way.*

Robert's womanizing ways came to a head in 1931 when he met Eula Mae Williams and her friend, the sixteen-year-old Virgie Mae Smith, on a trip back to Hazlehurst. Captivated after seeing Johnson perform on the streets, Eula Mae and Virgie would sneak out at night to visit the rougher juke houses where Johnson played after the sun went down. They were not the only young women vying for Robert's attention—a handsome young blues singer who is new to town can feel at times like a rooster in a hen house—but their persistence paid off, and Johnson and Virgie began a casual relationship.

Driven partly by desire and partly by jealousy, Johnson could barely leave his new girl alone, having sex with her in the woods while Eula Mae and her own boyfriend looked on and meeting her for flings in the morning before school. A few months later, Virgie fell pregnant. According to Eula Mae's account, Robert was excited by this news, perhaps looking on this as a second chance to build a family after the first had been taken away, and even offering to take Virgie with him to Memphis with the hope of starting a new life with the Spencers. Whatever Robert's dreams, they were not to be. Virgie's family was religious and did not consent to the union. The child Claud was born on December 12, 1931. He never knew his father. In 1998, after living his life as a truck driver, Claud was found by the State of Mississippi to be Johnson's legal heir based on Eula Mae's testimony. He died a wealthy man in 2005, aged eighty-three, and by all accounts used his lately acquired wealth to benefit his community.

On May 4, 1931, Johnson married again, this time to Caletta "Callie" Craft, a woman who was at least eight years Johnson's senior, in Hazlehurst, Mississippi. It is reasonable to presume that this marriage was at least in part an attempt to make Virgie jealous. While we may speculate that his first marriage was an attempt to settle down as an honest man, there was clearly no similar intention in this second union. Robert appeared to consider his new wife little more than a meal ticket and continued his flirtations and affairs throughout their relationship, even briefly hooking up again with Virgie. Craft doted on Robert all the same; however, she soon fell ill. She and Robert moved to Clarksdale, where Robert abandoned her in short order. She died in 1934. It is not known if Robert was aware of her death at the time or even if he would have cared if he had known. He certainly appears to have made no effort to visit his wife after she had outlived her usefulness to him.

Helena, Arkansas lies in the heart of the Mississippi Delta, an easy half-hour drive from Clarksdale and a short trip to Memphis. It has been a hub of the blues since at least the early 1930s, providing an easy base for artists whose work took them to both sides of the Mason-Dixon line. As the home of the *King Biscuit Time* radio show, it plays an important role in the history of the blues. *King Biscuit Time* is to the blues what the *Grand Ole Opry* is to country music, a freely accessible format with a loyal following that exposed the music and its performers to a wider audience than could ever be achieved through live performance and record sales. First broadcast in 1941, *King*

Biscuit Time was an important platform for artists including Rice Miller, better known as the second of two artists to go by the Sonny Boy Williamson moniker, Pinetop Perkins, and the man who we will see can lay genuine claim to being Robert Johnson's heir, Robert Lockwood Jr., who was also known as "Robert Junior" due to his association with Johnson.

After abandoning Callie Craft, Johnson made a base for himself in Helena. It was here, or through contacts gained here, that Johnson met the likes of Sonny Boy Williamson, Elmore James, Honeyboy Edwards, and Johnny Shines. If his time with Ike Zimmerman was his university, this was graduate school. The relationship between the musicians was one of peers: They all learned from one another to the degree where it can be hard at times to know for certain who influenced whom. Even a cursory listen to the extant recordings of the named musicians shows how each of them took a common musical vocabulary and adapted it to their singular voice. When listening, for example, to Elmore James perform "Dust My Broom," it is as much his song as it is Robert's, even if Johnson's recording precedes James's by over a decade. It is likely here that Johnson met Johnny Temple, who stated that he learned the boogie-bass rhythm of his salacious *Lead Pencil Blues* from Johnson. Johnson learned to mask his playing style, positioning himself to hide his hands and facing the wall whenever he thought another musician was watching his playing a little too closely in order prevent such stylistic theft from happening again.

Johnson soon found himself shacked up again, this time with Estella Coleman, although the relationship was never formalized by a minister or judge. Johnson took a shine to Coleman's son, Robert Lockwood Jr., and the two soon entered into a mentorship relationship that in many ways mirrored the earlier relationship of Johnson and Zimmerman. Although Johnson was normally protective of his playing style, he was more than willing to share what he knew with Lockwood, encouraging the boy to first build and then buy a guitar and teaching him signature techniques, such as the boogie-woogie runs that imitated the sounds of the barrelhouse piano.

Johnson was now being noticed and respected as a blues musician. He had a career and a reputation, as well as the respect of his peers. He was making his mark in the world, as seen by the imitation of Johnny Temple and the fact that he now saw fit to pass what he had learned on to the next generation. But he still lacked in one area. If he really wanted to break into the big time and become a known person, he had to record.

If influence correlated to fame, H.C. Spier would be a household name. A man of many and diverse business interests, it was in his role as a talent scout for the major record companies that he made his biggest impact. Spier owned an electronics store in Jackson, Mississippi. Situated in the hub of the African American business district, Spier had a strong line selling instruments, record players, and records. He paid close attention to what his customers were both buying and searching for, putting him in a unique position to see coming trends and audition artists on behalf of Columbia, Paramount, Okeh, and others. He was good at his job. Through his discoveries of important artists such as Skip James, Charley Patton, the Mississippi Sheiks, and others, Spier shaped the sound of recorded blues and helped capture the first recordings of songs that would become blues and later rock 'n' roll standards.

In 1936, Johnson traveled to Jackson to audition for Spier. Spier owned a small recording machine that he installed in a ramshackle studio above his store, leaving the tantalizing possibility that he recorded Johnson as part of the audition process. Sadly, any such recording, if one was made, is lost to the mists of time. In any case, the rehearsal was deemed successful, and Johnson was recommended to Don Law for recording and release through the American Record Corporation (ARC).

Johnson's first recording session took place in room 414 of the Gunter Hotel, San Antonio, Texas, on November 23, 1936. The hotel still stands today in the same location. As was typical practice at the time, the label aimed to get as much product as it could from its hotel booking. As well as Johnson, hillbilly and Mexican artists were included in the run of recordings, including the legendary songstress, Eva Garza. The session was produced by Don Law, an experienced producer of blues, hillbilly, and other folk styles who had a reputation for creating records that would sell. He knew that, when recording these styles, the artist knew his audience better than he did, and that his role was to make the artists comfortable and act as a guide to the recording process, rather than to be a hands-on producer and arranger. It is from Law that we get the anecdotes surrounding the recording process, including the famous story, depicted on the cover of *King of the Delta Blues Singers*, that Johnson was so shy he would only play while facing the wall.

By this stage in his career, Johnson was an experienced performer, used to playing for crowds, often playing in the street where his style could be seen in full view. It is unlikely that his facing the wall was due to nerves. It has been suggested that Robert was protecting his style and was eager to prevent future incidents like what had happened with Johnny Temple. In a 1990 interview with *Guitar Player* magazine,[5] Ry Cooder raised the possibility that Johnson was "corner loading," using the acoustic properties of the corner of the room to boost the middle and bottom ends of his guitar sound. If this is the case, it suggests that Johnson was familiar with adapting his sound for the recording studio and raises the tantalizing possibility that Johnson had recorded previously in similar circumstances. If this is the case then, just like the possible Memphis record booth recordings and H.C. Spier audition, they remain waiting for an enterprising researcher to track them down.

Johnson's understanding of the recording process is also indicated by the quality of his songs and arrangements. The Delta Blues style is one that grew up in the juke joints and house parties, where the purpose was to keep the song and driving beat going as long as possible, to keep the dancers dancing, the drinkers drinking, and the gamblers gambling, with the aim of making the performance of benefit to the organizer and ensure repeat bookings. This extended style was unsuited to the three-minute time limit on a 78 rpm record. Listening to the recordings of other Delta musicians, you can see they struggled with the time constraints of the recording studio: Songs are hurriedly finished up when the recording time nears an end, on occasion split into two sides of a record (most notably with Charley Patton's "High Water Everywhere") or else are compiled of "free" or "floating" verses strung together over the blues form, allowing the singer to bring the song to a quick end once the red light went on, indicating that the recording was reaching the three-minute mark. Johnson's recordings were different. Learning his lessons from the urban blues, jazz, and popular tunes he had picked up in his travels, Johnson ensured his songs tolda complete story within their limited time span, with a musical and lyrical beginning, middle, and end. Often the openings were based on a traditional theme or motif known to the audience, which was then developed in new and surprising ways. Even a song like "They're Red Hot," built on a repeating, circle of fifths chord progression inspired by ragtime and early jazz, used tricks like different vocal timbres and rhythmic variation that added shades of light and dark, giving a sense of tension and release to the arrangement of a song that could otherwise have become repetitive and outstayed its welcome on record, however successful it may have been in front of a live audience.

Close listening shows that Johnson was aware that performing for record was a different beast from performing live, and he arranged his songs accordingly. One of the more interesting outcomes of this careful arrangement is the fact that most of Johnson's "twelve-bar blues" in fact comprised longer choruses, usually thirteen bars in total, with an extra half measure being added to the start and end of each verse to allow for intro and outro guitar fills, while still keeping the timing of each verse consistent. While it was typical for rural blues guitarists to vary their choruses' length and add extra measures to their so-called "twelve-bar" blues as required—John Lee Hooker and Lightnin' Hopkins being two of the most notorious examples—it was rarely done in the consistent manner that Johnson did. Once again, Johnson showed acute awareness of the difference between recorded music and live performance, and leaving us with the tantalizing possibility that he had relevant prior experience in the recording studio.

A MEETING AT THE CROSSROADS: ROBERT JOHNSON AND THE DEVIL

It is worth taking a moment to discuss the suggestion that Johnson's recordings were sped up by the record company. A number of articles, mostly circulating online, have raised the possibility that the recordings we have are some 20 percent faster than Johnson actually played, having been manipulated in an attempt to achieve a more commercial sound. Digital files have been circulated with the reduced speed in an attempt to show how Johnson "really" sounded, and CDs of these slowed-down versions have even been made commercially available, albeit without the permission of the Johnson estate. There are a number of reasons to doubt this theory. The most compelling is that those who knew Johnson and heard him play never commented on this fact. The rumor only seems to have been able to take hold after those who were able to safely contradict it were long gone. In addition, the suggestion of a consistent speed change is doubtful. All up, Johnson recorded five sessions over seven months. Recording machines of the day were primitive compared to the rapid advances in recording technology over the '40s, '50s, and '60s, especially the portable systems used in *ad-hoc* hotel room studios. To suggest that the recording speed could be adjusted so consistently over multiple sessions on temperamental equipment stretched the bounds of credulity. We also have the evidence of the alternate takes. The record company may have found "Come On In My Kitchen" too slow, but rather than speeding up the first take, the second take was recorded with Johnson playing at a faster tempo. Ultimately, this theory tells us more about perceptions and stereotypes of the blues, the idea that this is slow music of heartache and pain and that a song recorded at a fast tempo, or with a danceable beat, must be the result of error or manipulation, than it does about Johnson and his music.

As was typical practice at the time, Robert was paid a flat rate per side recorded and did not receive any royalties from future sales. This arrangement suited both label and artist. For the label, it kept their costs fixed and allowed them to easily offset the losses of poorer-performing records, while for the artist it meant a guaranteed payday instead of vague promises of an unknown amount at an unknown future date. Many artists found this arrangement so suitable that some, such as Lightnin' Hopkins, continued to insist on upfront payment right up to the end of their career. In contrast, others, with John Lee Hooker being the most notable example, took advantage of the situation to record under pseudonyms for labels beyond their contracted home to fatten their bankroll.

The recording session was deemed a success. The first release from the session, "Terraplane Blues," backed with "Kind Hearted Woman Blues," was a reasonably sized hit. While exact sales numbers are hard to determine, estimates range between five and ten thousand units sold. The listenership was even larger. As jukeboxes represented one of the major markets for blues releases at the time, a single copy had the potential to reach dozens, if not hundreds, of listeners. Later releases, including "32-20 Blues" / "Last Fair Deal Gone Down" and "I Believe I'll Dust My Broom" / "Dead Shrimp Blues," were less successful, selling only in the low hundreds; however, working on the formula of one hit record paying the way for ten less successful releases, the session punched above its weight. Johnson was certainly proud to have not only records, but a bone fide *hit* under his belt.

Honeyboy Edwards recorded an incident when Johnson, while busking in the streets, received a request for "Terraplane" and proudly proclaimed, "Lady, that's my song," before playing to the appreciation of the crowd and receiving a hefty helping of tips as thanks for being the originator of a local favorite tune[6]. "Terraplane" was the first of Johnson's songs to inspire a cover version, recorded by Georgia bluesman Frank Edwards (1909-2002) in 1941 for the Okeh label.

Johnson's second recording session was booked for June 19 and 20, 1937, again with Don Law in the producer's chair. Scheduling necessitated that this time the session take place farther south in Dallas. The recordings released from this session included future standards "Hell Hound on My Trail" and "Stop Breakin' Down," but nothing repeated the sales success of "Terraplane."

One hit was enough. Robert was a recording artist who had proven he could shift records, and his music was being heard by more people than ever could have heard him playing live. Having had a hit also meant he could earn more money on the road, either through playing the song he was known for, or just from the extra bargaining power earned through being a bona fide recording artist and the prestige that came with the territory.

It is likely that about this time, Johnson first encountered the newly invented electric guitar. When playing noisy jukes and house parties, the electric guitar would have seemed a godsend to the performer keen to be heard above the background noise of conversation, fights, and dice games. Unfortunately, the amplifiers' temperamental nature, the less portable nature of the guitar and amplifier combo, and the lack of electricity in the rural areas where Johnson commonly played meant that he did not stick with the electrified instrument. If he had lived, Johnson would likely have been part of the electric blues revolution led by the likes of Elmore James and Muddy Waters.

Unknown to Johnson, his reputation was already beginning to spread further and wider than he could have imagined. White record collectors had noticed his music and were already starting to spread the word of this obscure blues performer who, by their measure, played with a power and composed lyrics with poetry that was unmatched in the genre. Slowly, plans were being made to track down Johnson and share his music with the wider public. Sadly for us, although perhaps to the benefit of the growing legend, they were too late.

In July or August of 1938, Johnson's travels took him to the outskirts of Greenwood, Mississippi. He took an offer to play over two consecutive Saturday nights at a convenience store *cum* juke joint called Three Forks, probably located some ten miles out of the town itself.

According to the most commonly accepted story, Johnson had taken a fancy to the wife of the owner of the juke, and this attention had been reciprocated in kind. When Johnson returned the following Saturday to complete the second engagement, the owner in a fit of jealousy, offered Johnson a bottle of liquor that had been poisoned with strychnine. Johnson became ill and was unable to perform his second set. By around two in the morning, he was laid out on a bed. What happened afterward has been the subject of much mythmaking and speculation. According to Sonny Boy Williamson's account, Johnson spent his final moments crawling on all fours and howling like a dog before dying in Sonny Boy's arms. Other accounts have Johnson's condition slowly deteriorating over a number of days. Despite these discrepancies, all accounts agree that Johnson died in convulsions and great pain.

The exact cause of death is impossible to determine. The official death certificate, written by the Leflore County Registrar, reads on the reverse:

> *I talked with the white man on whose place this negro died, and I also talked with a negro woman on the place. The plantation owner said this negro man, seemingly about twenty-six years old, came from Tunica two or three weeks before he died to play a banjo at a negro dance given there at the plantation. He stayed in the house with some of the negroes saying he wanted to pick cotton. The white man did not have a doctor for this negro as he had not worked for him. He was buried in a homemade coffin furnished by the county. The plantation owner said it was his opinion that the negro died of syphilis.*

As no autopsy was performed, we can cast reasonable doubt on the syphilis diagnosis. While Johnson was a known womanizer and could likely have carried the disease, the diagnosis was often applied at the time to African Americans who died of unknown causes based on prevailing myths and cultural attitudes. We can see the lack of care in the claim that Johnson was playing the banjo. No doubt the Registrar's office did not know nor care that Johnson was a guitar player. The banjo suited the stereotype of an African American musician, so banjo it was.

Despite the rumors, we cannot be certain that Johnson's death was the result of murder. Even if we accept that Johnson drank poisonous whiskey, the moonshine that was served at such events could be highly variable in quality, ranging from quality product made by bootleggers who cared about repeat customers to rough rotgut made with dirty equipment, laced with traces of dangerous chemicals and perhaps flavored to mask the taste. Accidental poisoning is as likely as deliberate murder.

Johnson's body was promptly buried in the days following his death. He may have sung about burying his body by the highway side, but even that fate would have led to more certainty about his final resting place than we currently have. According to the death certificate, Johnson was buried in an unmarked grave in a "Zion Church" in Leflore County. Unfortunately, for those wanting certainty regarding Johnson's final resting place, Zion is a common church name in the South, and memorial stones for Johnson have been erected in three different Zion churches matching the description.

And so ended the life of Robert Johnson and the beginning of his strange afterlife. It wasn't long before two events would take place that would begin to cement his reputation as, just like the record tells us, the King of the Delta blues singers.

From Spirituals to Swing

In 1938, record producer John Hammond (Sr.) hosted the "From Spirituals to Swing" concert in New York's Carnegie Hall. As the title indicates, the intent of the concert was to show the development of African American music from its very beginnings to the then-contemporary sounds of big band jazz and swing. Performers included the Golden Gate Quartet, Big Joe Turner, Mitchell's Christian Singers, Sister Rosetta Tharpe, and the Count Basie Orchestra. The country blues was represented by Sonny Terry and Big Bill Broonzy (himself perhaps a better example of the uptown, urban sound popular in Chicago at the time but readily adaptable to more rural styles if the situation and paycheck called for it).

The intent was also to include Robert Johnson. Hammond was familiar with the Johnson records then available and considered him the apex of the style. Hammond and his agents attempted to track Johnson down and arrange for him to perform at the show; however, they soon discovered that their star performer had recently died. Not wishing to cancel the scheduled appearance, at the appointed time during the concert, Hammond took the stage and made the following speech:

> *Robert Johnson was going to be the big surprise of the evening. I knew him only from his blues records and the tall, exciting tales the recording engineers and supervisors used to bring about him from improvised studios in Dallas and San Antonio. I don't believe that Johnson ever worked as a professional musician anywhere, and it still knocks me over how lucky it is that talent like this ever found its way to phonograph records. At the concert, we will have to be content with playing two of his records; Johnson died last week at the precise moment when Vocalion scouts finally reached him and told him he was booked to appear at Carnegie Hall on December 23. He was in his middle twenties, and nobody seems to know what caused his death.*

Following this introduction, in place of a live performance, two Johnson songs were played on stage via phonograph to an enraptured, if perhaps slightly confused, audience, "Preaching Blues (Up Jumped the Devil)" and "Walkin' Blues."

If you want to turn a man into a myth, this has to be the textbook way to go about it. "From Spirituals to Swing" was packed with big names: Benny Goodman, Big Joe Turner, Big Bill Broonzy, and Count Basie were all established hitmakers and major concert draws in their own right. This was *it*, the best of the best, the hitmakers, pioneers, trendsetters, and innovators, the kind of performers who could take a tradition and create something new and exciting out of it without stepping outside of it. These were artists with a reputation. The concert's appeal and promise were not just to see all these artists together on the same bill but to see them in the context of the evolution of the cultural and musical traditions they shared. And on top of all that, there was one artist that almost nobody, not even the most dedicated aficionados, had heard of, the one who promised to be the Rosetta Stone, the tablet that translates the field hollers into the language of Count Basie and back again. And then the rug gets pulled out from everyone: He's not here; we tried to get him; he's dead and gone, and all that remains are records and a ghost.

I don't want to go suggesting that the concertgoers left Carnegie Hall talking about the Devil and the crossroads and all that. But one idea was definitely and definitively planted: Johnson as the one that got away, the great talent cut down in his prime. Based on Lomax's hagiographic speech and the haunting image of the phonograph playing on stage, and no doubt also because the two records that were played were so damn good, Robert Johnson left his mark on the minds of everyone there. His records were still obscure, hard to find, and mostly known to collectors, but he was now a known quantity, already tied to a story. The great artist, gone too soon, the one-in-a-million find taken away before he could receive his reward.

The Muddy Waters Plantation Recordings

In 1941, the folklorist Alan Lomax was traveling the South collecting recordings of traditional and folk musicians on behalf of the Library of Congress. In August, his travels took him to Stovall's Plantation, Mississippi, some ten miles out of Clarksdale. Asking the locals about blues singers of note, they directed him to the home of a twenty-six-year-old tractor driver and blues singer named McKinley Morganfield, better known by the nickname given to him by his grandmother, "Muddy Waters."

The resulting recordings, made on an unwieldy and heavy early portable recording machine, are remarkable for two reasons. The first is the quality of the music. Muddy may have been young, but he was an experienced performer with a mature, developed style, and on tunes such as "I Be's Troubled" and "Country Blues," the listener can hear the Delta style that Muddy would take to Chicago, electrify, and so revolutionize not just the blues but all popular music. Some of the songs recorded would remain in Muddy's repertoire for his entire career, right up until the Blue Sky recordings produced with Johnny Winter in the late '70s.

Secondly, the recordings are accompanied by brief interviews in which Lomax asks Waters about the songs and his influences. In these interviews, Muddy clearly cites two major influences on his style: the elder musician Son House and Robert Johnson, clearly stating that he learned to play the song he called "Country Blues" through imitating Johnson's recording of "Walking Blues."

Lomax returned for further recordings in July 1942 and eventually sent Muddy copies of the recordings on disc. Throughout his career, Muddy maintained that it was through hearing himself on record that he gained the confidence to travel to Chicago and play his country blues in the urban environment. It is difficult to imagine the history of blues and rock 'n' roll if Muddy had not made this crucial change.

Through being cited as an influence by such an important figure, Johnson was elevated from being merely an excellent singer, songwriter, and performer. He now took on the role of an influence, a pioneer, the cornerstone that sits at the center of the history of the blues. One could draw a line from the early country blues singers such as Charley Patton straight through Robert Johnson to the Chicago blues of the '50s, onwards to the West Side sound of Otis Rush and Magic Sam. If one desired (and many did), one could even continue on to rock acts such as The Rolling Stones and Jimi Hendrix, creating a history of popular music with Johnson firmly in the center.

[1] Dylan, 2004, p282

[2] Conforth, 2008
[3] ibid
[4] ibid
[5] Obrecht, 1990
[6] Palmer, 1982, p129

The Crossroads and The Blues Tradition

I walk on pins
I walk on needles
I walk on gilded splinters
Just to see what they can do[1]

The Georgia-based blues singer "Cousin" Leroy Rozier (1925-2008) was not one of the giants of the blues. He was not a significant hitmaker, and his discography is limited; although some of his tunes, such as "Up the River" and "Waiting at the Station," became sought after by popcorn and rhythm and blues DJs. In 1960, his song "Crossroads" was released on the Herald label as the B-side to "Waitin' at the Station." Originally recorded in 1957, and featuring "Champion" Jack Dupree on piano, the song, built on a modal, single-chord melody, tells us about an encounter at the Crossroads:

> *Well I walked down by the crossroads*
> *There I learn how to play my guitar*
> *Well a man walked up, said 'Son, let me tune it'*
> *That was the Devil*
> *That was the Devil*
> *Oh lord now*
> *Oh well now*
> *Sho' nuff*
> *Oh lord now*

A MEETING AT THE CROSSROADS: ROBERT JOHNSON AND THE DEVIL

...

Oh well well my baby
Walked up to my door
'Will you tell me, where did you learn?'
Well I walked down by the crossroad
That's where I got my lesson
That's where I got my lesson
Oh lord now
Sho' nuff now
Alrighty now

Here we have it, the whole story, laid out before us, lacking only Robert's name, immortalized on wax even before the wide availability of Johnson's music on *King of the Delta Blues Singers*. If anyone was asking for it, here is clear evidence that the tale of the Crossroads was out there as part of the blues tradition, independently of Johnson and his later fame.

Based on musical themes derived from the same tradition as Robert Petway's "Catfish Blues" and Muddy Waters's "Rollin' Stone," it is quite clear that this is a bragging song, a boast of the same school as tunes like Bo Diddley's "Who Do You Love" and Willie Dixon's "Hoochie Coochie Man." By boasting about not just his prowess as a bluesman but the diabolical source of his skill, the singer is making two things very clear: that the life of a bluesman is one sanctioned by Satan and not by God and this decision can be represented by the Crossroads.

Like so much else within the blues, the symbol of the Crossroads has its roots in the church and spiritual music. Listening to William S. Hays's 1875 Jubilee spiritual "Angels Meet Me at the Crossroads," we hear:

Angels meet me at the crossroads, meet me
Angels meet me at the crossroads, meet me

THE CROSSROADS AND THE BLUES TRADITION

angels meet me at the crossroads, meet me
Don't charge a sinner any toll

In this song we can see the beginnings of the blues form as a theme is stated, repeated, and followed up with a closing statement. The spirituals, along with the work songs, the music of the minstrel stage, and the raucous sounds of the gambling dens, brothels, and drinking houses, is part of the traditions that fed into the music that we call the blues, and here we can see that the crossroads is a part of this early tradition.

While it is an angel, not a Devil, that is met at the Crossroads, the one going down to the Crossroads is still a sinner, and it is at the Crossroads that he is given the opportunity to make a choice between mending his ways and accepting salvation of continuing a life of wickedness and misdeeds. Johnson's stepsister Annye C. Anderson recalls a sermon on this theme by her aunt's husband, the Reverend Cross. In this sermon, which we can reasonably suppose Johnson had the opportunity to hear, the preacher tells us how "at the crossroads, you must make a decision, determine if you're going to be a Christian and believe[2]." Similar themes were common in other preachers' repertoires, and even when the Crossroads motif was not specifically called out, the theme can be heard in sermons such as the Rev J.M. Gates's "Are You Bound For Heaven Or Hell?", which uses the railway motif to illustrate the choice between the righteous and the sinful path. The idea of a choice made between virtue and vice being made at the Crossroads is even older. The story of Hercules being wooed by the spirits of virtue and vice at the Crossroads is an old one, dating at least to the time of Xenophon (c430-354 BCE), and was a popular motif in Renaissance art.

A recording of "Angels Meet Me at The Crossroads" was made in 1916 by the actor and blackface minstrel performer Harry C. Browne. Browne specialized in adapting minstrel and spiritual tunes for his unflattering stage and film depictions of African American life. He is best known for his adaptation of "Turkey in the Straw" with new title and lyrics, which is considered by some to be the most racist song in American music. That Browne chose to cover "Meet Me at the Crossroads" shows that the song and its theme were common enough in the African American tradition to be a meaningful target for parody. The song has proven resilient enough to survive to the present day, and we can find it in the repertoire of contemporary gospel and vocal groups. Echoes of the song can also be heard in Bone Thugs-n-Harmony's 1996 hit "Tha Crossroads."

In the forms of Pentecostalism most commonly practiced among African Americans at the time, salvation could only be found through faith in Christ and baptism in the Holy Spirit. Unless a choice has been made to accept Christ as savior, salvation is unobtainable. For the believer, the preacher, and the gospel singer, this is the meaning of the Crossroads, the decision to travel down the road to eternal reward over the more tempting roads that inevitably lead to certain damnation.

The Crossroads theme is a natural one to adapt for blues, inverting the formula to celebrate choosing the life of sin and barrelhousing over the good Christian life. Using the crossroads in this way perhaps goes back to the very beginning of the music. As we saw earlier, W.C. Handy's first encounter with the blues was hearing a local playing slide guitar at a railway station and singing about going "where the Southern cross the Dog." The Dog was the colloquial name for the Yazoo and Mississippi valley railway line, also known as the "Yellow Dog," while the Southern was the name for the network of railway branch lines that created the consolidation of numerous branch services in 1894 and ran from Washington and St. Louis in the North down to New Orleans and Jacksonville. Railroad crossings commonly allow trains to slow down, so that the traveler could jump on board and, depending on the direction they have chosen, go to a life of faith or a life of sin.

Variations of the motif of the "Southern crossing the Dog" were common in the early blues, and it is difficult to say for certain if this grew from the folk tradition, as heard by W.C. Handy on that fateful day at the railway station, or from familiarity with Handy's adaptation of the lyrics in his 1914 publication "Yellow Dog Blues." Southern Mississippi blues guitarist Sam Collins recorded his own tune called "Yellow Dog Blues" in 1927, although this tune bears no musical or lyrical resemblance to Handy's composition. In it, Collins sings:

> *Be easy mama, don't you fade away*
> *Be easy mama, don't you fade away*
> *I'm goin' where the Southern Cross the Yellow Dog*

The crossing of the railway lines represents an escape, a leaving, and also a decision to live the type of itinerant life associated with traveling musicians.

Moving from Southern Mississippi to the Delta tradition, in 1929's "Green River Blues," Charley Patton sings:

> *Think I heard the Marion whistle blow*
> *I dreamed I heard the Marion whistle blow,*
> *And it blew just like my baby gettin' on board*
>
> *I'm goin' where the Southern cross the Dog*
> *I'm goin' where the Southern cross the Dog*
> *I'm goin' where the Southern cross the Dog*

Patton visited the crossroads theme more explicitly at the same recording session in "Joe Kirby Blues":

> *I was standin' in Clack's crossroads, biddin' my rider goodbye*
> *I was standing at the crossroads, bid my rider goodbye*
> *It blowed for the crossroad, lord, she started to fly*

As in the gospel tradition, the crossroads is a place to change direction, an opportunity to either change the way one is going, or, if one continues down the path, it is a choice and not a matter of circumstance.

We can see the Crossroads motif outside of the Delta in the music Texas blues singer Will Day, who makes explicit reference to the crossroads in 1928's "Central Avenue Blues":

> *Boy I'd better see my good girl, leave me in this town*
> *I'd beat the train to the crossroads and I'd burn the depot down*

Will Day's lyrics appear to draw from the same tradition as Ramblin' Thomas's "Hard Dallas Blues," also recorded in 1928:

> *And before I would stand to see my baby leave this town*
> *I would beat the train to the crossing and burn that doggone bridge down*

The development of this theme continued into the post-war electric era. When Elmore James recorded his "Standing at the Crossroads" in 1954, he was not covering Johnson so much as creating a unique song from within the same tradition. Other than the opening line, the song shares almost nothing directly with Johnson's song. Using the same driving boogie and slashing slide guitar riff as Elmore's earlier hit "Dust My Broom," itself a much closer rendition of the Johnson song with which it shares a title, Elmore sings about standing at the Crossroads, being lost and lonely, and searching for his baby.

In James's recording, the Crossroads is explicitly a state of mind and not a real place. Elmore is not at a railroad crossing or highway junction any more than Dante was genuinely lost in a dark wood. Yet the meaning is clear: The song represents a person whose life has reached a junction; Elmore is working within the same tradition as Johnson but, for all his undoubted talents, is unable to take the Crossroads motif and relate it to concrete experience in the same manner as Johnson.

The examples shown make it clear that by the time Johnson recorded "Cross

Road Blues," the Crossroads were already a recognized theme and motif in the blues tradition. Motifs like this were part of the blues singer's trick bag, functioning as a kind of shorthand allowing them to set the theme for the performance right at the beginning and also providing a jumping off point for lyrical and thematic improvisation and variation: traditional motifs, including "Smokestack lightning, bell shine like gold", "I wish I were a catfish, swimming in the deep blue sea," and "I'm going to saddle up my pony, saddle up my black mare." These motifs can appear in the beginning, middle, and end of the song and allow the singer to pack maximum meaning into the twelve-bar form. When Son House adds the traditional milk cow motif at the end of "My Black Mama," he is using the traditional form to turn the song on its head and turn it from a celebration to a lament.

When Johnson opened up "Cross Road Blues" by telling us that he'd gone down to a crossroads and fallen down on his knees, he could trust his listeners knew what he was singing about. They've heard the songs, heard the sermons; they know that this is a place where sinners go to choose the road to Heaven or the road to Hell. Johnson is venturing into known territory. He proceeds to both invert and expand the theme in the second verse, where he sings about trying to flag down a ride. Here, the familiar motif is brought down to earth, and it is revealed that the song isn't about a spiritual crossroads as the audience may have expected; it's about a traveler out on the road. Johnson's audience in the juke houses where he played, and where his records were on the jukebox, would have often been in a similar situation themselves. Things get darker in the next verse as he sings about the sun going down.

Here, Johnson is singing about real danger. In Mississippi and elsewhere, an African American on the road after dark could find himself in genuine peril. So-called "sundown towns" could be found across the United States, where non-white people found outside after dark would be arrested, if they were lucky, or lynched if they were not. Roadside signs with warnings such as "Nigger, don't let the sun set on you here,"[3] were a familiar sight to the rural traveler. We can imagine Johnson's audience laughing uncomfortably at the line that describes a very real danger in their lives.

In the next verse, Johnson namechecks Willie Brown. The name would have been well known to Johnson's local audience, carrying with it the whiff of the jukes and the rambling life of the bluesman. At the crossroads between life of salvation or sin, Johnson is showing his cards and choosing to sink down rather than rise up.

In the first take of the song, the one that the producer chose for release, Johnson includes one final verse. This close verse reflects the emotional state of both a lonely hitchhiker and perhaps the spiritual state of the crossroads, looking west and east, lonely and with nobody willing to help.

And we're done. Not even two minutes of music, just a few short verses and we have a powerful statement that uses the existing structure and motifs of the blues, mixed with unique embellishments, to tell us something that is at once personal and universal. Johnson's artistry creates something that speaks to us powerfully even today. To Johnson's audience, already familiar with the meaning of the crossroads through sermon and song, Johnson spoke directly to them and of their choice to prioritize a Saturday night in the juke joint over more pious duties on Sunday morning.

Over the years, Johnson's song has become a standard. In 1968, a rocked-up version was a worldwide hit for the British supergroup Cream. Since then, there are few blues bands that don't have it in their repertoire. It brings in the tips and can be adapted to please both casual blues-rock fans and Delta blues purists. We've also seen how a parallel family of Crossroads songs grew up. Elmore James may have run in the same circles as Johnson, but it is difficult to call his "Crossroads" a cover of Johnson's original in the same way that "Dust My Broom" is.

The Devil

Who is the Devil that Johnson is said to have sold his soul to? While the Devil in the blues tradition shares many traits with the traditional Christian Devil, he acts in opposition to the Christian God; he rules over Hell and generally functions as a perfectly capable Prince of Darkness. Despite this, he is a figure distinct from other depictions of the Devil. Unlike the purely malevolent Devil of the fire-and-brimstone preachers, the Devil of the bluesman has positive traits and serves as a breaker of social and physical bonds. While we can draw comparisons with spirits and gods from African and Afro-Caribbean traditions, like the blues itself, he cannot be reduced simply to what came before. He is his own self, born on American soul out of the same cross-cultural mixing, blending, and creation that gave us the blues.

Syncretism is the name given to the process of merging and blending of religious and spiritual traditions, often brought about by the engagement and interaction between different cultures. The Romans were masters of the art, readily identifying the gods of conquered cultures with their own deities. We see it also with the Christian saints, who often have their origins in the gods or spirits of non-Christian cultures. Many patron saints in Ireland and Britain can be identified with Pagan deities, and even Gautama Buddha makes an appearance in the popular medieval collection of the lives of saints *The Golden Legend* as Saint Josaphat. We can see a recent example of medieval and Christian syncretism in action in the Mexican death-saint Santa Muerte, who combines aspects of the Catholic Virgin Mary with pre-Colombian death gods to create a figure of worship that is wholly new. A more extreme example can be seen amongst the Kastom people of Vanuatu, some of whom recognize the late Prince Phillip, the Duke of Edinburgh, as a divine figure.

The Devil of African American folklore is one such syncretic figure. He combines the attributes of the Christian Satan with figures from African religion and folklore. Elements of the spirits and loas of Afro-Caribbean religions, themselves examples of the blending of African and Christian traditions, can also be found. Unlike the malevolent force of Catholic and Pentecostal Christianity, the tragic hero of Milton or tempter described in the Gospels, this Devil is closer to the Trickster archetype. The Trickster is a mythic figure first identified in studies of Native American folklore, typified by characters including Coyote, Crow, and the Hare. We will explore the Trickster further in the next chapter; however, it is important to understand that unlike the wholly evil Satan, the Trickster Devil is a more ambiguous figure, neither wholly good nor wholly bad, who falls afoul of his own schemes as often as he triumphs. In folklore, the Devil can represent either the defiant African American hero or the oppressive landowner, depending on the story's needs. The Devil can be both an enemy and an ally. He is powerful, and if you have him on your side, you can do great things, but he is also tricky and difficult to trust.

In one typical African American folk tale, a young girl called Milandy is approached by the Devil who offers her a pretty dress and a pail full of milk. In exchange, he asks that before she turns thirty, she will give him her soul. Time passes and sure enough the girl reaches her thirtieth birthday and the Devil comes to collect. Unfortunately for the Devil, the contract is purely verbal, and Milandy is able to fulfil her end of the bargain by giving the Devil the sole of her shoe.

In the story of Jack and the Devil, the titular Jack is a bad man: a drinker, a gambler, and so forth. The Devil decides that any man that wicked surely has a place in Hell and knocks on Jack's door to collect the soul he considers rightfully his. Jack makes one last request, a drink of whiskey for the road. Having drunk everything in his house, Jack and the Devil head to the local tavern but Jack is caught short and cannot pay for his drink. He convinces the Devil to turn himself into a coin that can cover the tab, after which he can transform back into his infernal form. Rather than paying for his drink, Jack promptly shoves the coin into his pocket where the Devil is trapped by the crucifix already there, and Jack lives to sin another day.

We need to keep this figure of folklore in mind when we listen to blues songs that name-check the Devil. He is to be feared, yes, but the wily and watchful person can out him. In the right circumstances, he can even be a powerful ally. He acts as a mirror to the people who interact with him. He reflects their cunning, their trickery, their sins, but also their virtues.

Pre-war blues often featured songs about this Trickster Devil, a figure who can stand outside of and poke fun at social norms. We've already seen the example of Clara Smith's 1924 tune "Done Sold My Soul to the Devil," in which she declares:

> *I done sold my soul, sold it to the Devil,*
> *And my heart done turned to stone*
> *I've got a lot of gold, got it from the Devil*
> *But he won't leave me alone*

Here, Smith is claiming her place outside of the rules of polite society. While there is some element of just deserts for such a choice as her heart turns to stone and the Devil takes her soul, the song's overall mood is one of celebration rather than lament. If the Devil is the price to pay for such freedom, then so be it. In this way, the song is a sister tune to songs such as Bessie Smith's "Young Woman Blues" (1926), where the singer celebrates her newfound freedom at the loss of her man or Lucille Bogan's depiction of prostitution in "Groceries on the Shelf (Piggly Wiggly)," where she declares, "My name is Piggly Wiggly and I swear you can help yourself / You've got to have your greenback, and it don't take nothin' else".

In 1928's "Devil's Gonna Git You," Bessie Smith sang:

> *I don't want no two-time stuff*
> *From my regular man*
> *Don't want nothing that's been used*
> *'Cause it's second-hand*

A MEETING AT THE CROSSROADS: ROBERT JOHNSON AND THE DEVIL

The Devil's gonna git you
Oh the Devil's gonna git you
Man the Devil's gonna git you
Sure as you're born to die

The song is addressed to an unfaithful lover. Here the Devil is the spirit of what we might today colloquially call karma, the fallout that comes from making the wrong choice. Bessie Smith's father, William Smith, was a part-time Baptist preacher, and here she is, taking the language of her father's sermons and recontextualizing it. Even in the world of freedom portrayed in Smith's songs, actions have consequences, and the Devil can dispense justice in his realm as thoroughly as God can in His.

For Smith, the Devil could also be a positive force. In "Black Mountain Blues" (1930), she sings about how she's got "The Devil in my soul," while in "Send Me To The 'Lectric Chair" (1927) she tells us:

I want to take a journey
To the Devil down below
I done killed my man
I want to reap just what I sow
Oh judge, judge, lordy lordy judge
Send me to the 'lectric chair
Judge, judge, hear me judge
Send me to the 'lectric chair
I love him so dear
I cut him with my barlow
I kicked him in the side
I stood here laughing o'er him
While he wallowed around and died

There's no regret here for her actions and no sense that going to the Devil's realm is a punishment.

The Devil ruled over the urban nightlife as much as the rural. John Lee Hooker's 1949 recording "Devil's Jump" (released under the *nom-de-disc* "Texas Slim," although no attempt is made to disguise Hooker's unique vocal and guitar style) is a celebration of the freedom granted by the urban nightlife, echoing Hooker's earlier smash hit "Boogie Chillen." As the son of a preacher, Hooker grew up knowing what music belonged to the Devil and what belonged to God. His father, the Reverend William Hooker, only allowed religious music in his household. Things changed when his parents separated, and John Lee began to learn from his mother's new partner, the blues singer Will Moore. We hear this tension between the respected and the wild life echoed constantly in Hooker's "Boogie Chillen'" family of songs, which usually begin with the maternal command not to stay out at night.

Despite his love of earthly things, The Devil acts as a spiritual figure. He loves the blood and sweat of juke joints, whiskey houses, and brothels, but his body is spiritual, and his natural home is Hell. For an equivalent human figure, we need to travel to the brothels and buckets of blood to meet the bad man they call Stagger Lee.

The Bad Man Stagger Lee

In a pivotal moment in Craig Brewer's 2006 film *Black Snake Moan*, the fallen former bluesman Lazarus undergoes a kind of resurrection on stage. Performing at a local juke joint for the first time in years, he strums the guitar, steps up to the microphone and starts singing a song about wading through water, wading through mud and murder that went down at a place called the Bucket of Blood.

The story being told is an old one, one that has been told in song by artists ranging from the folky Mississippi John Hurt, the soulful Wilson Pickett, and, in a memorable performance from his *Murder Ballads* LP, Australian goth-rocker Nick Cave. It is the story of Stagger Lee. Sometimes spelled Stack Lee, or Stack O'Lee, he is the archetypal black badman, a man who revels in his sinfulness, and in some versions of the tale, his reputation is powerful enough to overthrow the Devil himself. Stagger Lee is the man who celebrates his wicked life because he knows respectable society has no place for him. He slays Billy Lyon, who represents this life, echoing the wild man Cain murdering his settled brother Abel, and the Egyptian Trickster god of the wilderness, Seth, murdering the agricultural god Osiris. Like Johnson, Stagger Lee started in history, became wrapped up in folklore and myth, and examining one can give us clues to the meaning behind the stories told about the other.

Stagger Lee was a real person, an African American pimp who plied his trade in nineteenth Century St. Louis. His real name was Lee Shelton, his nickname supposedly derived from the *Stack Lee* riverboat, well known as a home of prostitution. On Christmas night, 1895, he shot and killed William Lyons. A contemporary newspaper account in the *St. Louis Democrat* tells us:

> *William Lyons, 25, a levee hand, was shot in the abdomen yesterday evening at 10 o'clock in the saloon of Bill Curtis, at Eleventh and Morgan Streets, by Lee Sheldon, a carriage driver. Lyons and Sheldon were friends and were talking together. Both parties, it seems, had been drinking and were feeling in exuberant spirits. The discussion drifted to politics, and an argument was started, the conclusion of which was that Lyons snatched Sheldon's hat from his head. The latter indignantly demanded its return. Lyons refused, and Sheldon withdrew his revolver and shot Lyons in the abdomen. When his victim fell to the floor Sheldon took his hat from the hand of the wounded man and coolly walked away. He was subsequently arrested and locked up at the Chestnut Street Station. Lyons was taken to the Dispensary, where his wounds were pronounced serious. Lee Sheldon is also known as 'Stag' Lee.*[4]

Shelton was convicted for his crime in 1897, sentenced to twenty-five years in prison and released on parole in 1909. He returned to jail two years later and died of tuberculosis on March 11, 1912.

Perhaps due to the antagonist's colorful nature, the story quickly passed into folklore and into the repertoire of the early blues. Versions of the song were heard around St. Louis in the late nineteenth century. The first known recorded version was an instrumental reading by Fred Waring's Pennsylvanians in 1923. The first version with lyrics was Love Austin's "Skeeg-A-Lee Blues" in 1924. In 1925, Ma Rainey recorded a version with a different melody and lyrics, featuring Louis Armstrong on cornet. Rainey sings:

> *Stack O'Lee was a bad man, everybody know*
> *And when they see Stack O'Lee comin', they'd give him the road*

It's barely a decade after his death and Stagger Lee has, like Johnson would in his turn, passed out of history and into the world of myth. We have no reason to think Rainey was aware of the historical figure that the song was based on. Stagger Lee's name has become shorthand for the heroic bad man whose antinomian ways are to be celebrated. Like John Shaft and the heroes of Blaxploitation cinema, he's reclaiming his personal and cultural identity by exalting a willingness to act outside of law and custom, sometimes to achieve a just or righteous goal but always in the act of defiance. Stagger Lee is the prevailing culture's worst nightmare, the man who refuses to stay in his place, whose very being threatens the laws of Jim Crow.

Outside of the written and recorded histories, Stack was also becoming a hero of oral myth. Toasts are a form of African American folk poetry, usually telling the story of an anti-hero who uses his abilities or wit to find his way out of an extraordinary situation. Popular subjects of toast include the Signifying Monkey and a reimagined version of the bluesman Peatey Wheatstraw as well as Stagger Lee. In these tellings, Stagger Lee takes a further step away from history, able to take on the Devil directly. It is here that the antinomian aspects of the story are developed to their fullest. In one version we hear:

> *The Devil said 'Look, Stackolee I heard you'd a pretty bad man in that*

upper land,
But you know you're down here and met another bad man.'
Said, 'Okay Devil, you get your pitchfork and let me get my two smokin'
forty-ones
And two of us bad motherfuckers'll have us some fun.'
The Devil got his pitchfork and Stackolee got his two smokin' forty-ones,
And those two bad sonofabitches did have some fun
Stackolee shot the Devil right through the heart[5]

In some versions, such as Pacific Gas & Electric's 1970 recording, Stagger Lee deposes the Devil and becomes the ruler of Hell. Stagger Lee escapes even the final judgment. In life, he shackles off the laws of man; in death, he disregards the rules of the preacher.

Stagger Lee's shooting of Billy Lyon echoes many classic primal murders found in world myth. Like Cain killing Abel or Seth slaying Osiris, Shem the Penman and Shaun the Postman, the figure of civilization, of settling down or, for want of a better word, respectability is laid low by a wild spirit that questions these values. Stagger Lee may not have been a blues man, but he occupies a similar place in folklore. He is a celebration of choosing the carnal over the spiritual, a figure of such vitality that even when his final judgment comes, he finds a way to conquer Hell and continues his ways. He is the bluesman's freedom, the fulfillment of the choice at the crossroads, a man who can travel from town to town, live outside conventions and still triumph. He is an urban figure, but one that can break the laws that separate the city from the wilderness. He is an echo of an old archetype, the Trickster who lives outside the law. We see this archetype echoed in Robert Johnson's photo with a scowling face and a cigarette, and when he sings "Me and the Devil walkin' side by side." It is in this space that we start to see the face of the god of the Crossroads.

THE CROSSROADS AND THE BLUES TRADITION

Dealing with the Devil

But what of the deal with the Devil? Here is preacher LeDell Johnson's story, told to researcher David Evans in 1966, of his brother Tommy Johnson's trip to the Crossroads:

> Now if Tom was living, he'd tell you. He said the reason he knowed so much, said he sold hisself to the Devil. I asked him how. He said, 'If you want to learn how to play anything you want and to play and learn how to make songs yourself, you take your guitar and you go where the road crosses that way, where a crossroads is. Get there, be sure to get there just a little 'fore twelve o'clock that night so you'll know you'll be there. You have your guitar and you be playing a piece sitting there by yourself. You have to go by yourself and be sitting there playing a piece. A big black man will work up there and take your guitar and he'll tune it. And then he'll play a piece and hand it back to you. That's how I learned to play anything I want.' And he could.

The first thing to note is that this story is not repeated by any of Tommy Johnson's other relatives. This is not a retelling of an event that happened by a person familiar with the facts. Whether Tommy recounted the story to LeDell or if LeDell was pulling it from his own imagination, it is clear that the story functions on some level in the realm of myth or metaphor. It is not a description of a known encounter at a genuine crossroads (we can note that the crossroads itself is only described in the most general terms—there is no indication that this is describing an actual place but rather a generic or archetypal location), but rather a description of an inner state of the soul.

Now, Tommy Johnson was not what one would call a God-fearing person, and his life was dedicated to the path of the hard-playing, hard-living bluesman, the kind of person who would strain cooking fuel for alcohol if the situation called for it. When we look at the story with this in mind, we can more clearly see the intent behind LeDell's telling. His message is simple: Tommy Johnson was a bluesman, and to be a bluesman is to be a sinner, in league with the Devil. He may have been a great musician, people may want to know his story, but by living the life he chose, he gave up his soul for damnation. In this telling of the story, we get the message loud and clear: To live as a blues man, even a great one, is to turn one's back on God and to become part of the Devil's party. You don't sell your soul to become a blues singer. There's nothing to sell. By living a life of sin, you have stripped your soul of any value it may have once held.

The two Johnsons, Tommy and Robert, aren't the only famous bluesmen to have claimed a supernatural source for their musical ability. Howlin' Wolf had deep roots in the pre-war blues scene, seeing and performing with artists such as Patton, House, and Johnny Shines. In their biography of Howlin' Wolf, *Moanin' at Midnight*, Segrest and Hoffman document a conversation with the Wolf's son Floyd Frazier, who said his father would tell him a story of taking a guitar at nighttime to a cemetery and sitting on the grave of somebody he had known when they were alive. According to Frazier's account, the Wolf claimed that at midnight a man came and took his guitar, played a few chords, and handed it back to the Wolf and said to him, "Play!" After that, according to Frazier's account, the Wolf was able to head straight to a house party and play well enough to keep himself in fish and whiskey all night[6]. The authors note that Frazier appeared unfamiliar with the story of Robert Johnson.

Stories of the Devil at the crossroads can be found scattered throughout blues culture and African American tradition. Tales abound of musicians, sorcerers, and conjurers heading outside of town to come face-to-face with the Devil. Even the noted author and anthropologist Zora Neale Hudson is supposed to have had an encounter at the Crossroads, after being instructed in the process by a hoodoo doctor[7].

In February and March of 1960, the folklorist Frederick Usher Jr. met and recorded Eddie "One String" Jones and Edward Hazleton, two itinerant bluesmen he encountered in Los Angeles's skid row. Jones played the one-string diddly bow while Hazleton played the harmonica in the rhythmic, rural style typified by musicians such as Sonny Terry and Deford Bailey. Usher's recordings of these two musicians can be found on the LP *One String Blues*. After a performance of the country blues number "Throw a Poor Dog a Bone," Hazleton tells us the following story about country blues guitarist Blind Boy Fuller (1904 or 1907 -1941):

> *And that when I met the guy that trained Blind Boy Fuller to play on the guitar. And he told Blind Boy Fuller that he must go in this ... in the crossroads. A Crossroads. Do you know what a crossroads is? It's a crossing, you know, it's way out in the subs of town. It's called a crossroad. And he told him to go out on this crossroads for nine Sunday mornings before day. And, according to what this man told me, that he went out in this crossroads for nine Sunday mornings before day and on the ninth Sunday morning he came out playing anything and everything he wanted to play, and more than what he wanted to play just came right toward him.*

Blind Boy Fuller is best known today for his 1936 side "Truckin' My Blues Away," which contained the refrain "Keep on truckin'," later adapted by cartoonist Robert Crumb and adopted as a slogan by the '60s counter-cultural movement. Fuller later collaborated with Sonny Terry, and his style was an inspiration for a whole school of country blues guitarists, including Brownie McGhee, who first recorded as "Blind Boy Fuller No 2." This is the only known reference to Fuller engaging in any sort of satanic pact or crossroads ritual.

A meeting with the Devil at the crossroads doesn't just have to be about the guitar. In his monumental study *Hoodoo - Conjuration - Witchcraft - Rootwork*, clergyman Harry Middleton Hyatt collects a number of African American folk beliefs about the crossroads. To take one example, collected in Ocean City, Maryland:

A MEETING AT THE CROSSROADS: ROBERT JOHNSON AND THE DEVIL

> *If you want to know how to play a banjo or a guitar or do magic tricks, you have to sell yourself to the Devil. You have to go to the cemetery nine mornings and get some of the dirt and bring it back with you and put it in a little bottle, then go to some fork of the road and each morning sit there and try to play that guitar. Don't care what you see come there, don't get 'fraid and run away. Just stay there for nine mornings, and on the ninth morning there will come some rider riding at lightning speed in the form of the Devil. You stay there then still playing your guitar, and when he has passed you can play any tune you want to play or do any magic trick you want to do because you have sold yourself to the Devil.[8]*

We can see here a number of points of departure from the story associated with Johnson, mapping more closely to the story Edward Hazleton told about Blind Boy Fuller. The ritual is done in the morning rather than midnight and has to be performed over a sequence of nine days rather than on a single night. But significantly, the power of the crossroads rite is extended to give the ability to play the banjo as well as the guitar and to "do magic tricks." It is difficult to tell from this account whether the intent is to learn conjuring or actual occult ritual; however, the point may be moot as either activity can be used to ill ends, and neither is the mark of a respectable person.

Another example from Hyatt, collected in North Carolina, includes the details of the Devil tuning the guitar for petitioner:

> *You go out there [to the forks of a road] about four a'clock, jis' commence dawnin' day, jis' about crack of day, an' start a-pickin' at de guitar. Yo' go jis' onest. An' they says de Devil came out an' take it—jis' somepin will pull it from you, you jis' give up to it. An' he'll tune up an' hand it back to you and you start to play. You can pick any song you want to pick.[9]*

The power of the diabolical pact to bestow musical prowess isn't just limited to the guitar and the banjo but can include the fiddle or even the accordion.

> *There was a man who wanted to play an accordion, and he didn't know how to play it. And someone told him that if he would go to the forks of a road nine Sunday mornings in succession, one after the other, at four o'clock, and on the ninth morning if he could stand what he saw, he would be a musician. So he went those periods of time, and the last morning as he went across the field, he heard a noise. When he was sitting in the forks of the road, he heard an accordion playing a long time before it got to him. He said the accordion was about the size of a horse-cart body. He was coming across the field playing the accordion.*[10]

These instruments—the guitar, the banjo, the accordion, and the fiddle—are all associated with the rowdiness of the dance hall and the juke joint rather than the church. The fiddle in particular has long had associations with the Devil, beginning in medieval times to Paganini right up to Charlie Daniels's 1979 hit "The Devil Went Down to Georgia." The fact is that the Crossroads rituals collected by Hyatt extend further than the guitar, but remain limited to instruments as well as activities, such as gambling and magic, that are considered outside of the domain of God. And God-fearing folk ties the Crossroads pact not just to the blues but to a type of antinomian behavior, disregarded for cultural norms and taboos.

Zora Neal Hurston describes the Crossroads pact in detail in her study *Hoodoo In America*, published in the *Journal of American Folklore*. The pact is given the heading "How to Have a Slick Hand With People," and requires the practitioner to dress in black, sit at the Crossroads at twelve midnight, and sell himself or herself to the Devil, although it is not mentioned if the Prince of Darkness himself is expected to make an appearance. After doing this, the new initiate is granted the power to do "anything you wish to do."

The above examples show us that the idea of the crossroads was not introduced by over-enthusiastic blues fans hoping to lend their favored artist a touch of mystique to match the feelings they felt were conveyed in the songs. It was already an established part of the blues tradition. This is the tradition that Cousin Leroy was drawing on when he recorded his song in 1957 and the tradition that was being referenced when similar stories were told about Robert Johnson.

Sources conflict as to whether the Crossroads story was ever associated with Johnson in his lifetime. Some of those who knew him best, such as Johnny Shines, Robert Lockwood Jr., and Honeyboy Edwards, have for the most part denied the story, as does Annye C. Anderson. Son House's testimony is ambiguous at best, and it seems likely he is using the term as an expression, much as we might say somebody has got the Devil in them without expecting them to be genuinely possessed by a spirit. This has led many researchers to state that the story became associated with Johnson after the fact, with the song selection on *King of the Delta Blues Singers* providing a whiff of the supernatural, and once the Tommy Johnson story gets thrown into the mix with House's tales of Johnson's disappearance, the myth begins to grow. Yet, between all this we get some tantalizing hints that the tale is older than had been suspected. In a 1994 interview with journalist Paul Trynka, Honeyboy Edwards tells us that after his initial attempts to play the jukes, Robert "... went off, I guess of to the Crossroads. He told me he went to the Crossroads ... He probably did say that to frighten people ... Robert was a big bullshitter man,"[11] while in the 1992 documentary, *The Search for Robert Johnson*, two of Johnson's former girlfriends, Queen Elizabeth and Willie Mae Powell, both tell us they heard the story straight from Johnson. Mack McCormick tells us that the story was already in circulation among record collectors at the time of the *Spirituals to Swing* concert[12].

We can reconcile this by going back to what we said at the beginning: The crossroads isn't an event; it's a way of being. If it was said about Johnson that he sold his soul, or if he said it about himself, then it is a description of Johnson as a bluesman. We saw before how the crossroads symbol was used in sermons, in spirituals, and in blues to describe the point where one has to choose between God and the Devil. Johnson had chosen to live as a bluesman, which means, as far as he and most around him were concerned, in his own spiritual crossroads encounter he had turned his back on God and taken up league with the Devil.

The gap between the bluesman's life and the life of more respected folk is highlighted by Alan Lomax in his monumental study *The Land Where the Blues Began*, where he tells us, "In fact, however, every blues fiddler, banjo picker, harp blower, piano strummer, and guitar framer was, in the opinion of both himself and his peers, a child of the Devil.[13]" When John Lee Hooker started learning guitar from his sister's boyfriend, the bluesman Tony Hollins, his preacher father, the Reverend William Hooker, wouldn't allow the music in the house:

> ...I had to keep it out in the barn. All that time I was pluckin' on it and my daddy called it the Devil ... They all feel like it Devil music back then. They call blues and guitar and things the Devil's music ... Not only my father, everybody thought that. The white and the black ministers, they thought it was the Devil's music.[14]

One cannot be a bluesman and also a proper member of the community. The choice has to be made between blues and the Devil or the righteous path and God. We see this reflected in the words of Sterling McGee, a former '60s sideman who played with the likes of James Brown and Big Maybelle. Sometime in the 1970s, he stopped answering to his given name and insisted on being addressed as Mr. Satan, later becoming half of the duo Satan and Adam. Explaining the reasoning behind this change of name, he says it is "because my mother was a Christian it was a sin for me to play the blues. I'm serving The Devil."[15] Fat Possum recording artist Johnny Farmer tied this association directly to Robert Johnson. A laborer and bulldozer driver, Farmer was also an accomplished amateur bluesman and after much cajoling was able to be convinced to record and release the album *Wrong Doers Respect Me*. A reluctant performer, Farmer was convinced that while he could play the blues for his own amusement, to perform for others or record the music was a step beyond what was safe. When interviewed in the documentary film *You See Me Laughin'? The Last of the Hill Country Bluesmen,* Farmer describes this by explicitly invoking Robert Johnson. "Robert Johnson? Y'all know him? ... You see where he went to the Crossroads and stay there till twelve o'clock where the Devil play guitar and hand it to him? You see that? Well, that was actual truth, that was truth ... blues is the Devil's music.[16]"

More recently, we have the example of the "Mississippi Marvel," a church-going man with a sideline in playing the blues, who only consented to record and release his secular music on the condition of complete anonymity, given the scandal it would cause should his congregation become aware of his dalliances with sinful music. Even at the 2008 launch party for his album *The World Must Never Know,* the Marvel would only perform behind a screen that masked his identity. Such are the lengths taken to keep God and the blues each in their own place.

This split between the secular and the sacred existed throughout Southern culture, among both black and white communities. When Jerry Lee Lewis was in Sun Studio with Sam Phillips, working on a follow-up to his massive hit "Whole Lotta Shakin' Goin' On," the pull between God and the Devil became too much and he broke down, stopping mid-song, screaming into the microphone with a fervor that would make even his cousin Jimmy Swaggart seem mild and reserved, "H-E-L-L," spelling it out, "it says make merry with the joy of God *only* ... How can the DEVIL save souls? What are you *talkin'* about? Man, I got the Devil in me. If I didn't have, I'd be a Christian."[17] The threat of Hell and the Devil was as real to Jerry Lee as the keys on his piano. We see this repeated in the case of Jerry Lee's fellow '50s rock 'n' roll piano pounder Little Richard. While outwardly comfortable in his skin, Richard's flamboyant personality, along with his tastes in both drugs and men, clashed with his upbringing in charismatic and Pentecostal Christianity. In 1957, while on tour of Australia as part of a package show that included Gene Vincent and Eddie Cochran, Richard saw the newly launched Soviet satellite

Sputnik in the sky and interpreted it as a sign from God. At his next show, after being introduced to an eager crowd by Australia's own "King of Rock 'n' Roll" Johnny O'Keefe, Richard shocked both the crowd and the M.C. by walking out wearing white robes, carrying a Bible, and announcing, "Tonight, ladies and gentlemen, I'm not going to sing for you because I understand the end of the world is coming. I'm going to talk to you about the Lord." Instead of hearing salacious hits like "Tutti Frutti" and "Long Tall Sally," the audience was instead given a twenty-minute sermon on the imminent end times. Later in the tour, Richard tossed his diamond rings in the river and renounced rock 'n' roll. It was another half decade before he would record or perform the music that made him famous, instead dedicating himself to gospel music. For the remainder of his career, he would swing from the secular to the sacred and back again, before finally making peace with himself in the final decades of his life.

Despite this strong tension between the sacred and the secular, the blues and gospel genres shared many features in common. The music of the street preacher Blind Willie Johnson may sound like blues, but the intent is sacred, not secular; Blind Willie himself would not have considered himself a blues singer. The difference comes from the approach to the subject matter: The blues celebrates what the spirituals condemn, but the musical forms are similar enough that many artists could lend their hands to both genres if the situation called for it. Charley Patton recorded both sacred and secular music and was known to spend time as a preacher while Son House moved throughout his life between working as a preacher and playing the blues, often combining the two practices. After his rediscovery in the 1960s, he would often pause in the middle of a show, sometimes even mid-song, to preach a sermon to the crowd. But through all this you can sense that the two activities are considered fundamentally opposed. House expressed this internal conflict musically through his *tour-de-force* "Preachin' Blues," where the action in the preacher's tent and juke joint merge, becoming barely distinguishable from one another, and Son seems unable to tell if he is working for his salvation or damnation.

The traveling tent shows of the big blues singers such as Ma Rainey and Bessie Smith acted as a mirror image to the performance put on by the itinerant preacher. Both offered an escape from everyday life, a temporary moment of euphoria in which one could put aside their troubles and think of better things. The call and response interaction between the performer and the crowd were virtually identical, filled with cries of "testify" and "say it again."

Blues caters to carnal needs, not spiritual, and while there may be some who barrelhouse on Saturday night before attending the service on Sunday morning, it is not a thing to be accepted or encouraged. You can live a double life for a while, but sooner or later you've got to make a choice. We're back to the crossroads. You can choose to serve the Devil or the Lord, and it is made quite clear that the blues belongs to the Devil. And for those with spiritual needs that were not catered for by the church, there were other options available.

Voodoo, Hoodoo, and Conjure: Magic in the Deep South

Magical practices, whether labeled hoodoo, voodoo, or otherwise, were part of everyday life in Robert Johnson's South. Living in Memphis, the Beale Street that Johnson knew was full of not just music but magic. Spiritual supplies were readily available, whether in store or via a vast network of mail-order catalogs. Gamblers made sure they put on an extra splash of Hoyt's cologne before a game, hot foot powder was used to deter unwanted visitors, and mojo bags were so common that even President Woodrow Wilson was known to carry one to ward off his rheumatism[18].

Like the blues, the traditions of voodoo can trace their origins to Africa, but the traditions as practiced in the Americas were not born in Africa. They come from the blending of traditions from different parts of the old world in the new, where common ground could be found between African animism and European Catholicism, between shamanism and the Western magical tradition of the grimoires. The Vodun religion of the Fon people is a deeply animistic tradition. The world is alive, and natural phenomena are both ruled over and identified with living spirits. These spirits are numerous, including such as the mother-spirit Mahu, Xêvioso, the spirit of thunder and also of justice, and the previously discussed Legba, to more local spirits that have dominion over a single community or natural feature. In Vodun ceremonies, the practitioner, often aided by alcohol, will often allow the spirit to "ride" or possess them for the duration of the ritual, until the spirit is given a license to depart.

Vodun beliefs and practices, as well as the practices of other indigenous African traditions, traveled with their practitioners as they were forcibly transplanted to the New World. In the French Caribbean and French Louisiana, these spirits and animistic beliefs were able to make an uneasy synthesis with Catholicism, with practitioners finding parallels between their own practices and the Catholic beliefs of saintly devotion and intercession. This syncretism was particularly strong in New Orleans, where the line between Catholic and voodoo devotions can often be blurred. Marie Laveau, the famed "voodoo queen of New Orleans," was known to attend Mass each Sunday, the Catholic St. Expeditus has been transformed into the voodoo god St. Expedite, and rosary beads are often found on voodoo altars and sacred sites.

As they traveled throughout the United States, voodoo practices became more varied and eclectic, and practices could vary from state to state and from region to region. The eclectic nature of the practices is demonstrated by two of the most common spell books or grimoires commonly used by practitioners. *Pow-Wows; or Long Lost Friend* was first published in 1820. Compiled by the German American John George Homan, himself a member of the Pennsylvania Dutch community, and deriving from Germanic traditions of folk-magic, *Long Lost Friend* is a curious combination of spell book and farmer's almanac. As well as prayers to ensure a safe journey or to recover lost objects, it also includes recipes and is perhaps the only Western spell book to contain instructions for brewing beer. Curiously, despite its origins in the Pennsylvania Dutch communities and its popularity among practitioners in Mississippi and Tennessee, all strong Protestant and Pentecostal strongholds, the text of the book is clearly of Catholic origin, often invoking the trinity to bring about the desired magical effect. Spells cited in the book include the famous SATOR square, an arrangement of five Latin words that can be read forwards, backwards, vertically, and horizontally, examples of which can be found in the ruins of Pompeii and in the *Greek Magical Papyri*. The *Long Lost Friend* achieved notoriety in 1928 when it was found in the possession of one John Blymire, who had murdered a man by the name of Nelson Rehmeyer, believing the latter to be a witch who had placed a curse on him.

The apocryphal *Egyptian Secrets of Albertus Magnus* is a similar work to the *Long Lost Friend*, having its origins from the same Germanic tradition. The two works hold a number of spells in common, including a spell using the SATOR square as a means to quench fire without water. In a spell for making a scrying mirror, the practitioner is instructed to bury a mirror at the crossing of two pathways and leave it there for three days, imitating the time spent by Christ in his tomb. Recalling a common theme in folklore, including the tales told of the Devil's Bridge, which we will encounter in the next chapter, the mirror brings misfortune to the first person who gazes into it, and the practitioner is encouraged to show the mirror to a dog or cat before gazing into it themselves.

The *Sixth and Seventh Books of Moses* is an altogether different type of work, one that better matches the popular imagination's idea of a traditional magical grimoire. Filled with cabalistic symbols, magical circles, and words of power, the work presents itself as the secret writings and lore of nobody less than Moses himself. Citing the tradition that Moses was the author of the first five books of the Bible, the text offers itself as the sixth and seventh books containing the oral law delivered on Mount Sinai and not included in the *Pentateuch*. Describing itself as "The wonderful arts of the old Hebrews, taken from the Mosaic books of the Kabbalah and the Talmud," the text itself is typical of a eighteenth and nineteenth century magical text such as the *Red Dragon* or the *Key of Solomon* and appears to have largely used Francis Barrett's *The Magus* (itself largely derived from Cornelius Agrippa's *Three Books of Occult Philosophy*) as its source. It represents the traditions of so-called high or ceremonial magic, as opposed to the folk magic of the *Long Lost Friend*. Like the former work, the *Sixth and Seventh Books of Moses* seems to have also entered the American magical traditions via the Pennsylvania Dutch before being adopted into voodoo practices. Beginning in the 1920s, copies of the work found their way to West Africa, where they were openly advertised and sold and have now left their mark on Vodun and African witchcraft practices in their homeland.

Both these works were readily available in the various spiritual supply stores that could be found across the South or ordered through mail order catalogues serving practitioners who were unable to access a local source. Voodoo may not have been respected and, like the bluesmen, its practitioners may not have been looked on kindly by polite society, but it was hardly a secret or hidden current.

One other voodoo handbook deserves mentioning, and this one was even more readily available, easily picked up in any bookshop or hotel room: The King James Bible. Voodoo rituals often require the practitioner to recite verses, especially from the psalms. The importance of the bible to voodoo and root work practice emphasizes the syncretic nature of the tradition. A practitioner could invoke a spirit of West African origin using verses from the Christian bible while clutching a fetish ordered through the mail. If nothing else, voodoo was and still is about taking what was around you and making it work.

Voodoo doctors, root workers, and spiritual doctors were readily available for hire. Services offered varied from practitioner to practitioner, but generally included success in legal cases, the interpretation of dreams, the recovery of scorned lovers, removal of curses and bad luck, or, among the less scrupulous practitioners, the placing of curses and bad luck charms on one's enemies.

John the Conqueror is a figure that crops up in many parts of voodoo law. In early usage, he is a man, in some tellings an African prince who was sold into slavery and would pit himself against plantation owners and field bosses in battles of wits, always gaining the upper hand and bringing levity and laughter to the lives of his fellow slaves. Like Petey Wheatstraw, he finds himself falling for the Devil's daughter and earning the position of the Devil's son-in-law. Like King Arthur, John the Conqueror has never died but lies sleeping and will return when his people are once more in great need.

Magical themes have always played a part in the blues. Muddy Waters told researcher Robert Palmer, "You know, when you're writin' them songs that come from down that way, you can't leave something out about that mojo thing. Because that is what black people really believed at that time.[19]"

In "Mojo Hand Blues" (1927), Ida Cox, building a theme that would later be repeated by Muddy Waters and Lightnin' Hopkins, among others, said that she was:

> *Going to Louisiana, to get myself a mojo hand*
> *I'm going to Louisiana, to get myself a mojo hand*
> *'Cause these backbiting women are trying to take my man*

In 1928, Blind Lemon Jefferson told us in "Low Down Mojo Blues" that his current lover, his "rider," was:

> *Tryin' to fool her daddy, she's tryin' to keep that mojo hid*
> *She's tryin' to fool her daddy, she's tryin' to keep that mojo hid*
> *But papa's got something for to find that mojo with*

Moving ahead to the 1960s, Louisiana blues and R&B singer Charles "Mad Dog" Sheffield suffered from his lover's voodoo working, and Tabby Thomas could sing about a party thrown by the voodoo king and voodoo queen.

When used and referenced in song, the traditions of voodoo and hoodoo conjure up images of both humor and menace at the same time. Ida Cox was singing about taking control of her man and her love life, but she was also talking about genuine traditions and practices. A mojo was traditionally a charm bag, a *gris-gris*, filled with different ingredients depending on its desired effect. A mojo could win back a lover, bring luck in gambling, or drive away ill-fortune. As Blind Lemon tells us, to remain effective a mojo should be kept hidden, typically on one's person, and the finding or revealing of the mojo will reduce or negate its effectiveness.

One of the most famous blues songs to reference these practices is Willie Dixon's "Hoochie Coochie Man," first recorded in 1954 by Muddy Waters for Chess Records. Muddy tells us about charms such as the black cat bone and John the Conqueror root, singing of virility and sexual conquest, symbolized by known voodoo practices. For many outsiders, it is easy to see this as a song about something dark, dangerous, or secret. In reality, it was little different from a pop song mentioning astrology or perhaps Albert King's "Born under a Bad Sign." The song only makes sense if the listener understands the reference. Muddy's main audience was women, and he was selling them a fantasy using language they understood. This takes us back to the start of the chapter and Cousin Leroy's "Crossroads." The song only exists because the story it tells, of the crossroads and the Devil, is already known to its audience. Bad men, bluesmen, sell their soul to the Devil, and to make that claim in song one-ups any mojo hand or hoochie-coochie man.

Voodoo and mojo charms were a part of life but, like the blues, they weren't *respectable*. Spiritual doctors, charm dealers, and the like set up shops all over the South and beyond, offering success in law, love, and gambling. At their best, these practices carried a slight tinge of the forbidden; at their worst, you were risking your immortal soul. They run in parallel with the blues as something that is *of* the community but, of necessity, always to some degree *outside* the community. Practices such as spirit possession were an inversion of possession by the Holy Spirit and speaking in tongues, as practiced in Pentecostal services. In a culture where salvation is dependent on faith, choosing voodoo over the Church makes one's position very clear. The president may have had a mojo, dream books may have helped you play the numbers, but get serious about the practice and, as far as the Church is concerned, you've forfeited your eternal reward. Singing about hoodoo, mojo, and the like falls into the same category as songs about cowboys, pimps, hustlers, and so forth. It can be malicious or benign, but the underlying meaning is always clear. Like the blues, if you choose these practices, you're placing yourself in opposition to God and risking your eternal reward. We're back at those Crossroads again.

[1] Tallant, 1946, p21
[2] Anderson, 2020, p74
[3] Pearson & McCulloch 2008, pp. 76
[4] Wyman, 2001, p107
[5] Brown, 2003, p183
[6] Segrest; Hoofman, 2005, p62
[7] Huston, 1931
[8] Hyatt, 1970, p 104
[9] Hyatt, 1970, p108
[10] *ibid.*
[11] Gussow, 2017, p 214
[12] Gioia, 2008, p163
[13] Lomax, 1994, p365
[14] Mussay, 1999, p32
[15] *Satan and Adam*, 2018
[16] *You See Me Laughin? Last of the Hill Country Bluesmen*, 2002
[17] Guralnick, 2015, pp 370-371
[18] Kail, 2019, p13
[19] Palmer, 1981, p97

The God of the Crossroads

Ἑρμᾶς τᾷδ᾽ ἕστακα παρ᾽ ὄρχατον ἠνεμόεντα
ἐν τριόδοις, πολιᾶς ἐγγύθεν ἀιόνος,
ἀνδράσι κεκμηῶσιν ἔχων ἄμπαυσιν ὁδοῖο
ψυχρὸν δ᾽ ἀχραὲς κράνα ὑποϊάχει
  —**Anyte of Tegea**

The word "myth" is commonly used to describe something that is considered a falsehood. We talk of such things as urban myths and use expressions like "the myth of exceptionalism," but a myth can be so much more. A myth can be an ideal, a pointer toward a higher truth that lies beyond the trivialities of people and places and events, those things that belong squarely in the solid world of being. Myths can lead us to the ideas and ideals that lie behind the story and take us into the place where we find the truths that define our world, and from these truths that land of potential, of things that are still coming into being. We see this in the myths of the ancients and in more modern myths like the story of Faust or even the larger-than-life heroes of the Marvel Cinematic Universe.

Myths can be an attempt to describe the world. The myth of Zeus castrating his father Cronos shows us a vision of cosmic cycles and superhuman forces: the Biblical creation myth, the Indian Mahabarata, Mohammad's night journey, the tales of the Australian Dreaming, and so on. These are stories that describe the world on a scale larger than man, stories that steer our gaze beyond the horizon. The King Arthur of history was most likely a minor British warlord with a few successful campaigns under his belt, but the myth is something much more. It can teach us about chivalric ideals, national pride, and it can ask deep questions about the value of nationalism.

Myths defy attempts to find a single explanation. Efforts have been made to explain myth as a form of proto-science, as an extension of ritual, the products of the unconscious, as a form of literature, and on it goes. These different approaches can all provide momentary, albeit contradictory, satisfactory explanations of the same myth and provide a pathway toward deepening our understanding of the story. We may alternate between these approaches, or even apply different approaches simultaneously, without exhausting the depths of possibilities contained within the myth. Ultimately, myths provide us with a way of communicating fundamental truths about ourselves and the world around us.

Myths continue to be created. Figures arise, whether fictional like Superman or Luke Skywalker, or historical like Wyatt Earp, Elvis Presley, or Robert Johnson. These are figures who embody an ideal and who resonate on a scale large enough that they find themselves becoming part of the ongoing march of ongoing mythic forms, becoming part of the older stories and generating new stories of their own.

Read enough myths and repeated forms and motifs arise again and again. Diverse cultures speak of worldwide floods, of divine kings, and of gods who die and are reborn. Once it was supposed that these myths spoke to history, that the multitude of flood myths found, for example, reflected the reality of a historical deluge. Now we see the form that lies beyond the story, the archetype that gets repeated and retold, that provides a place for each culture to hang its clothes and create something new, retell the old stories in a new way, and to tell new stories in a way that can be understood. Again and again the old myths tell us of gods and kings, of death and rebirth, of miraculous births, the march of cosmic cycles, brother slaying brother, and on it goes. Look closely enough into the myths and we'll find the god of the Crossroads.

THE GOD OF THE CROSSROADS

The god of the Crossroads is the god of the outsider. He stands at odds with social norms, as much as he is a product of the culture that created them. Just as Crossroads are places "in-between," neither one place nor the other, so is the god of the Crossroads never strictly a hero or a villain, but always contains within him the capacity to be both. Crossroads are the intersection between the way you have come and the way you choose to go or, to put it another way, between what is and what may come into being. They are where the sacred meets the profane, where spirits descend to the Earth, and where mortal souls strive toward immortality. The Crossroads are an opening up of possibilities, just as in common speech a "crossroads moment" is an opportunity for choice, but with this possibility there is always the element of risk. The wrong path may be chosen or the traveler may not be properly prepared for the dangers they may encounter. In myth, to go to the Crossroads is to invite change and possibility. Crossroads are most typically found in the countryside and wilderness but are unmistakably a product of a settled culture. If you don't have permanent or at least semi-permanent settlements, you don't need roads in between them.

The god of the Crossroads is a subset of the Trickster archetype. The Trickster can be found across the world in myth cycles from the First Nations of North America, where he was first identified and named, to Africa, China, Australia, and more. Well-known Trickster figures include the North American Crow and Coyote, the Northern European Loki and Odin, the Chinese Monkey King Sun Wukong, and, in West Africa and the New World, Legba. The Trickster flouts social norms and bites his thumb at convention. While his antics and japes may come back to bite him, he is in all cases an instigator of change. He can have positive and negative aspects, but most of the time he doesn't make much of a distinction between the two. Change and disruption are his game; he leaves it to others to decide after the fact if what happened was good or bad. In African American stories we see his face in folktales about the Devil and in the stories told about Stagger Lee. The Trickster crosses boundaries, passes through gateways, and, in the cases that most interest us, he is met at the Crossroads. He can be a source of humor; he can triumph over great odds, but a price is often paid. The Wurundjeri people of Australia, whose traditional land includes much of the area now known as the city of Melbourne, tell the story of how their Trickster figure Crow used his tricks to steal the secret of fire from the seven Karatgurk women (represented by the constellation Pleiades). Sharing this secret with the other Dreamtime spirits, Crow lost control of the gift and caused a massive bushfire, which threatened the entire land. Eventually the fire was extinguished. Crow, however, was left singed, turning his feathers black. This is a typical Trickster tale; the Trickster changes the order of things, bringing gifts but also danger.

The Greek Trickster Hermes is best known as the messenger of the gods, and as the psychopomp, he guided souls down into the land of the dead. In addition to these duties, he was also the patron of thieves, the inventor of lying, the first to play a stringed instrument, and explicitly a god of the Crossroads. Herma, shrines to Hermes, could be found at crossroads and boundaries throughout the Greek world. Originally these shrines were just piles of stones left as offerings to the god by travelers. Eventually, they developed into a column of carved stone. Later still, the head and phallus of the god, placed at the appropriate height, were added to the form.

To learn more about Hermes and the kind of tricks the god of the Crossroads likes to get up to, we can travel back in time a bit to one of the very first stories told about him, the story of his birth as passed down to us in that odd collection of poems, prayers, and folktales called *The Homeric Hymns*. In the *Hymn to Hermes*, we are told how Hermes's mother, Maia, was a shy goddess, not comfortable in the presence of other immortals, and took to hiding herself away in a remote cave. As was his habit, Zeus found himself enraptured by her beauty, and slipping away from Olympus in the middle of the night he snuck into Maia's cave to have his way with her. Maia fell pregnant and in due course gave birth to the infant god Hermes. Being immortal and the son of the king of Olympus, Hermes was not like other babies. On his first day on Earth, only a few hours old, he was already walking and talking and soon decided to explore the world. While his mother is out, he leaves the cave and encounters a tortoise. He kills the tortoise and takes the body back to his cave, where he proceeds to hollow out the poor creature's shell, attach ox hide to act as a resonator, affixes sheep gut to act as strings, and he's made himself the first stringed instrument, a lyre. Naturally, he's pretty pleased with himself and starts plucking at the instrument and singing songs in honor of his father and mother and telling the story of his own birth.

Before long, young Hermes gets hungry and fancies the taste of meat. Not far from the cave, the sacred cattle that belong to the god Apollo are grazing. Hermes decides that this will make a pretty good meal, but he doesn't want to get caught. He makes himself a pair of sandals out of wicker to disguise his tracks, and taking fifty cattle from the herd, he drives them so that they will walk backward, their tracks facing the opposite direction to the one in which they are actually driven. While he is driving the cattle, he is spotted by an old man working in the vineyard, but Hermes buys the man's secrecy by promising a bountiful harvest come the appropriate season. Thus hiding his crime and bribing the only witness, Hermes gets the cattle near his cave, slaughters them, and builds a fire to roast them on. Being one of the immortal gods, he can't actually eat the flesh of the cattle, but he does enjoy the aroma of the cooking flesh. Once he's done, he puts out the fire, hides the bones, and runs back to his mother's cave, where he jumps back into his crib and starts acting like a newborn baby rather than the cunning cattle thief he's proven himself to be.

Apollo eventually notices the missing cattle and goes off in search of them. He finds the old man in the vineyard who, after realizing that he is in the presence of a god, breaks his promise to Hermes and admits that he saw a young child driving the cattle backward. Having learned of this ruse, Apollo is now able to follow the tracks and makes his way to the cave where Hermes and Maia live. Hermes is in his crib and starts crying and cooing just like a little baby should, hoping to throw Apollo off the scent. Apollo searches the cave for the thief and recognizes the signs that this isn't any ordinary cave but the home of immortals. Sensing a ruse, he accuses the infant Hermes of being the thief, who speaks back in his own defense, protesting that he is only a day old and clearly not capable of anything as audacious as cattle theft. Apollo, who has the advantage over Hermes of literally not being born yesterday, sees through the ruse and quickly recognizes Hermes as both a god and the thief. He demands that Hermes come with him to Olympus so that Zeus can arbitrate the case. Zeus is delighted by the whole situation, acting the role of the proud papa, praising his infant son for causing so much mischief on his first day on Earth. This puts off Apollo, but eventually, an agreement is reached. It is decided that as compensation for his missing cattle, Apollo is to be granted possession of Hermes's lyre. By way of recognition, Apollo's gifts to Hermes are a golden wand, which is not named in the original myth but can be recognized as the Caduceus, and the herald's staff often depicted with two snakes intertwined around a central pole. In order to give his son something to do with his time besides wanton theft, Zeus assigns to Hermes his twin functions as messenger of the gods and psychopomp.

In this story, we can clearly see the stratagems and tricks that are common signifiers of the Trickster god. While Apollo is the god commonly associated with the lyre, we see that Hermes invented the instrument, and he was the first to play music on it. The Crossroads have been associated with music and stringed instruments since ancient times. Hermes is also the inventor of the panpipes, further strengthening the link between the Crossroads and musicians. As the messenger of the gods, Hermes is the only figure who can travel freely between the realm of the gods, the underworld, and the mortal world. We are reminded of the Christian St. Peter, the keeper of the keys, commonly identified with Papa Legba in the various voodoo traditions.

The Greeks also considered the Crossroads sacred to the goddess Hekate, whose domains included the night, witchcraft, and necromancy. Common epithets for Hekate include "Hekate of the Three Ways" and "She who frequents the Crossroads." A three-branched Crossroads was one of her primary symbols, and, like Hermes, shrines to Hekate could commonly be found erected at rural boundaries and crossroads. She was very popular in late antiquity, and her aid is sought in many spells appearing in our most extant record of Greek magic and sorcery, the Greek Magical Papyri. In Virgil's *Aeneid*, she is famously evoked by the spurned Carthaginian queen Dido. Dido casts herself on her funeral pyre, cursing her departed love Aeneas, prince of Troy and legendary founder of the Roman people[1]. Hekate was also closely associated with the agricultural goddesses Demeter and her daughter Persephone and played a function in the initiatory Mysteries of Eleusis.

Hekate was associated with dogs. They were considered sacred to her and were commonly sacrificed to her. She was often depicted in art accompanied by one or more black dogs. In one story, Queen Hecuba of Troy leapt into the ocean on seeing the destruction of her city. Hekate took pity on this tragic queen and transformed her into a dog to serve as her companion. In other depictions, the dogs represent the restless souls of the underworld. Hekate's association with dogs is echoed in later depictions of diabolical hounds, from the "black dogs" of English folklore to Gothe's depiction of Mephistopheles appearing in the form of a poodle to Johnson's "Hellhound on My Trail."

In the Roman tradition, the crossroads were sacred to the fertility god Liber. Like Hermes, he was associated with the phallus and his shrines commonly encountered by travelers at Crossroads. His association with wild, orgiastic rites led him to be identified with the Greek Dionysus as well as with Hermes. His festival was the Liberalia, held on March 17th, which celebrated the transition from youth into manhood.

Not all Tricksters are gods. A Trickster can also be mortal, a hero figure who overcomes great odds, even defying the will of the gods, through cunning and stratagems. In the Greek tradition, this mortal, heroic Trickster can be most clearly seen in the Homeric hero Odysseus. Homer describes Odysseus as the "master of stratagems" and a "man of twists and turns." It was Odysseus who devised the Trojan Horse that allowed the Greeks to capture Troy and end their decade-long siege of the city. The ancient geographers

Strabo, Eratosthenes, and Apollodorus both supposed that Odysseus's famous voyage home took him beyond the world known to the Greeks and into the aquatic wilderness the Greeks called Ocean. While others supposed that Odysseus remained in the Mediterranean and attempts were made, even in ancient times, to identify the locations visited with known places—Virgil places the Cyclops, Scylla, and Charibdas near Sicily—it is agreed that the journeys take Odysseus beyond civilization and into the wilderness. The various adventures and encounters Odysseus faces share many features in common with the Crossroads symbol. The famous encounter with the Cyclops represents a contrast between the rustic, uncivilized life of the one-eyed giants ruled by their appetites and the settled life in Ithaca and other Greek cities. We see also the significance of choosing between the known and unknown life: Odysseus prevents Polyphemus from calling for help by claiming his name is "Nobody." When he drops this pretense and shouts his name at the beast, he allows Polyphemus to call down the curse that causes Odysseus to wander the seas.

Odysseus spends the last seven years of his voyage on the isle of Ogygia, the prisoner of the nymph Calypso. Infatuated with Odysseus, she offers him the gift of immortality, which he rejects. This is a moment of decision, the kind of thing we refer to as a Crossroads moment, the choice between a blissful immortality living in pleasure with a nymph, albeit as her prisoner, or rejecting the offer and returning home. For Odysseus, who has already traveled to and from the horrors of Hell, this cannot have been an easy choice. Note, also, that being of the mortal realm, having been to the Land of the Dead and returned, and having been granted access to life as an immortal, Odysseus is echoing Hermes's freedom of access to the realms of Being.

Leaving Ogygia, Odysseus navigates his way home by the means of the constellation of Ursa Major, the Great Bear. Rotating around the pole star, this is the only constellation that never dips below the horizon. Its path around the Celestial Pole is often represented by various cruciform figures, creating a crossroads in the sky.

THE GOD OF THE CROSSROADS

In the Roman world, Hermes was known as Mercury. In his dialogue *De Natura Deorum* ("On the Nature of the Gods"), Cicero, the Roman statesman, philosopher, and scourge of Latin students everywhere, depicts his speaker, Gaius Aurelius Cotta, discussing the various forms the gods take in Greek and Roman myth. In the text, Cotta identifies three different gods that can be called Jupiter, as well as four different Apollos. The different Mercuries identified include the son of Zeus and Maia we met in the previous story, and the Mercury who is described as the son of the Sky God and the goddess of the Day. Cicero describes two Egyptian gods who can be identified with Mercury. The first is the Ibis-headed god Thoth, inventor of the hieroglyphs, who ruled over magic, medicine, and the law. The second is described as a "Son of the Nile," whose name is not spoken by the Egyptians.

In Cicero's time, the Egyptian god whose name was not spoken was Seth, the slayer of Osiris. Popularly, Seth is often considered the villain of Egyptian myth, who through killing his brother brought death into the world. In popular depictions, such as in the films *Gods of Egypt* or the Tom Cruise vehicle *The Mummy*, he is reduced to an enemy or Devil figure. The Seth of Egyptian myth is a much more complex figure. Originally, the chief god of Upper Egypt, Seth ruled over moments of transition such as circumcision, birth, and, in the Pyramid Texts, the opening of the mouth ceremony which allowed the deceased to speak the spells that granted him passage into the afterlife.

Like Hermes, he was a god of borders and boundaries and was associated with the quick-moving planet Mercury. Hermes and Seth are both symbolized by the snake or serpent. Seth was unique among the Egyptian pantheon in that he was not readily identified with any known animal. While the other Egyptian gods are commonly depicted with the heads of known animals, Seth's animal is not easily identified. The Seth Animal, with its large ears, snub nose, and forked tail, has been variously identified with the donkey, aardvark, and fox, but it is likely that Seth is intended to be represented as a fantastic or imaginary creature, symbolizing his separation from the other gods.

Seth is best known for the myth cycle in which he slays his brother Osiris and contends with Osiris's son Horus. During times when the Osiris cult was in favor, Seth was reduced to playing the role of the opposition figure. During this period, Seth's name was not spoken, his statues destroyed, and his name erased from writings and inscriptions.

Seth also served as a preserver of cosmic cycles, accompanying the sun god Ra on his solar boat and slaying the serpent Apep, who threatened Ra on his nightly journey through the Duat. Like Hermes, Seth had functions to perform in the celestial, mortal, and chthonic realms.

Seth's association with the Crossroads comes from his rulership of boundaries and borders, of crossing from one place to another. Like Hermes, he is a patron of travelers and foreigners. He also was closely associated with the celestial crossroads formed by the movement of *Ursa Major*, known to the Egyptians as "The Thigh," around the Northern celestial pole.

In the Northern world, Hermes was identified with the one-eyed god Odin. Crossroads were sacred to Odin and were often cult centers and sites of ritual and sacrifice. In the old English sermon *De Falsis Diis* ("On the False Gods"), dating from the late tenth or early eleventh century, we are told:

> *There was also a man called Mercury; he was very crafty and deceitful in deed and trickeries, though his speech was fully plausible. The heathens made him a renowned god for themselves; at crossroads they offered sacrifices to him frequently, and they often erringly brought praise-offerings to hilltops, all through the Devil's teaching. This false god was honored among the heathens in that day, and he is also called by the name Odin in the Danish manner.*

In Norse myth, Odin functions as a positive Trickster in contrast to the largely negative Loki. He delights in cunning, trickery, and stratagems more than any of the other gods, even his son the wicked half giant Loki. Like the Greek gods, he often travels incognito, and any vagabond or traveler encountered on the road could secretly be the god in disguise. He commonly disguised himself as an old man wearing a gray cloak and a floppy hat covering his missing eye.

Odin is a seeker of the unknown. In one story, he lost his eye sacrificing it in the Well of Mimir in exchange for wisdom. The Old Norse poem *The Hávamál* describes how he learned the secrets of the Runes, by "sacrificing himself to himself," hanging for nine days from a tree that is unnamed in the poem but is accepted by most commentators as being *Yggdrasil*, the central tree that connects the Nine Worlds of Norse mythology.

> *I know that I hung on a wind-rocked tree,*
> *nine whole nights,*
> *with a spear wounded, and to Odin offered,*
> *myself to myself;*
> *on that tree, of which no one knows*
> *from what root it springs.*
> *Bread no one gave me, nor a horn of drink,*
> *downward I peered,*
> *to runes applied myself, wailing learnt them,*
> *then fell down thence.*

The act of hanging from the tree in this manner calls to mind a condemned man hanging from the gallows. Traditionally, in the European traditions, gallows are often placed at crossroads as protection from the spirits of executed criminals. Suicides were often buried at crossroads for the same reason.

The tree Yggdrasil stretched through all the nine worlds of Norse Mythology, from Asgard, the realm of the Gods, through the mortal realm of Midgard, the lands of the Frost Giants and Dwarves, down to Hel, the realm of the dead. Yggdrasil is an axial point and forms a Crossroads parallel to the one created by the Ursa Major's journey around the celestial pole.

Turning our eyes from the old world to the new, we travel to Haiti and the religion of Vodou. A product of the African diaspora, vodou grew out of a syncretism of the religions of West Africa with the Roman Catholicism of the ruling class. In Vodou, the Crossroads are sacred to the *loa* Papa Legba. Like Odin, Legba is often seen wearing a wide-brimmed hat. Like Hermes, he is a god of speech and language and acts as a messenger between Earth and spirit. Gates, keys, and doorways are also sacred to him. His equivalent in the Latin American Santeria traditions is Elegua. Often identified with St. Michael, Elugua is always invoked first in ceremony, and his permission must be gained before communication with the *Orisha* spirits is to be successful.

Haitian Vodou and Latin American Santeria are both products of syncretism between Catholicism and African traditions. Their roots can be found in the Vodun religion of the Fon people of West Africa, in the areas now known as Benin, Togo, and Nigeria. Here too, he functions as an intermediary and conduit to the spiritual realm. Like Hermes, he is a spiritual messenger. Like Seth, he is a cutter and a divider, one who marks the distinction between one thing and another, spatially and spiritually representing the boundaries between *this place* and *that place*. Again, his symbol is the crossroads, the boundary that marks the distinction between places and simultaneously opens up possibilities and multiple and alternate pathways. His shrines are commonly erected at doorways, entrances, and boundaries. Like Hermes, Legba is a phallic god often depicted with an erect and enlarged phallus.

In one story told by the Fon,[2] Legba is the child of Mawu, the feminine aspect of their androgynous and hermaphroditic creator god. As the lesser deity and servant, it is Legba who receives the blame when things go awry by Mawu, who receives the credit for good fortune. Naturally, Legba is unhappy with this arrangement. He tells Mawu that thieves are planning to raid her yam garden and steal her crop. Mawu is naturally upset about this and tells everyone that anyone caught stealing her yams will be put to death. That night, when everyone is asleep, Legba puts on Mawu's sandals, then helps himself to the plentiful yams. The next morning, Mawu is rightly upset and, spying the footprints, demands to examine the sandals of everyone in the village in order to identify the thief. When it is discovered that her sandals match those of the thief, Mawu is humiliated and forced to leave the Earth for the world above. Legba is left as her agent and intermediary in the world below. Mawu doesn't travel very far, however. Her heavenly dwelling point is only a few meters above the earth, and Legba is left to function under her watchful eye, forced to use his cunning if he wishes to act as an independent agent.

This story shares many features with the tale of Hermes and Apollo's cattle. Again, a child of a god, a Trickster and messenger symbolized by the crossroads, commits a theft by disguising his footprints. The Crossroads is associated with cunning and trickery, the figure who will do what is required to achieve his goals. Christian missionaries in Nigeria in the 1920s found that stories about Legba were being retold as being about Satan and the Devil; however, to their surprise, this did not carry the expected negative associations[3]. The Devil, as the other, the Trickster and questioner, is seen here not as the opponent but as an essential part of the order of things. In the context of the above story, it is the Legba, or the Devil, who rules things on earth and as such should be rightly approached and petitioned.

Eshu was the Trickster god of the Yoruba people. In one myth, he is responsible for upsetting the natural order by switching the place of the sun and the moon. Another story tells about the time Eshu walked down the road between wearing a hat that was red on one side and black on the other. The two friends who owned the neighboring farm began talking about this stranger and fell into quarreling when they could not agree on the color of the hat. One said that the stranger's hat was red, the other that it was black. Eshu eventually reveals himself as the source of the prank and confesses that causing discord and dissent causes him great delight.

The homelands of the Yoruba and Fon were hit hard by the slave trade. The Bight of Benin was a major slaving center, and it is estimated that by the late eighteenth century up to 30 percent of Louisiana's African-born population originated from this part of the African continent[4]. In this way, the figure of Legba was brought to the new world, where he entered voodoo and hoodoo traditions. He is a popular deity in New Orleans voodoo, where he is often given offerings of cigars, liquor, or candy in exchange for his assistance. As a god of crossroads, gates, and keys, he is commonly asked to assist in the removal of obstacles. He is associated with St. Peter, who in the Gospel of Matthew was given the keys to heaven[5], and St. Anthony, the finder of lost things.

You see what's going on here? A Trickster, a joker, a figure who rules over boundaries but also disregards them. Other gods may travel, but the god of the Crossroads is the one who makes his home anywhere he lays his head. Odin gains wisdom by sacrificing himself on the tree that passes through the Nine Worlds. What is bound on earth is bound in heaven, same with the loosening. Breaking through the boundaries, taking them down, making it so that at least in the brief moment they never existed at all, is his whole deal. The god of the Crossroads can be benevolent, he can be harmful, he can be both at the same time. Seth killing Osiris and preserving Ra are two sides of the same coin; defining the boundaries and borders between day and night, life and death, keeps the cycle going.

This dual nature can be seen in the Hindu crossroads god Bhariva. Like Hermes, shrines to Bhariva were commonly found at crossroads and often featured a prominent phallus. Bhariva represents the destructive aspects of the godhead Shiva. His form can be terrible, and he is often decorated in entwined serpents, again recalling Hermes's caduceus. Although he can be considered a fearful figure and his power most commonly manifests itself through destruction, Bhariva is also a great protector and his aid is often sought by those looking for a guru.

We see the dark side of the crossroads most clearly in the Central American Trickster Tezcatlipoca. Tezcatlipoca's cult was initially developed by the Toltecs and later embraced by the Aztecs, who embraced him as the patron deity of both kings and warriors. He was the primary creation god who offered his protection to rulers but was also associated with witchcraft and other dark arts. In Aztec myth, Tezcatlipoca introduced the practice of human sacrifice, through which the Aztecs believed they maintained creation, reviving the sun and keeping the fields fertile. In addition to the regular rounds of sacrifices that took place on a massive scale, the Aztecs would also choose a youth, typically a prisoner of war, each year to be Tezcatlipoca's representative on Earth for a year, living a life of luxury and honor, to be sacrificed at the year's end as the central rite in honor of their god of the Crossroads.

Like Seth, Tezcatlipoca was associated by his followers with the constellation Ursa Major and its journey around the axis point of the night sky. Corresponding to Seth's murder of Osiris, Aztec myth tells us how Tezcatlipoca corrupted his brother Quetzalcóatl, introducing him to sex and liquor and bringing about the end to the Golden Age. Like Hermes, Tezcatlipoca was a god of music, and the flute was particularly sacred to him. He could see the deeds and thoughts of all mankind and was known to appear at crossroads at night to challenge warriors and test their skill.

The name "Tezcatlipoca" means "The Smoking Mirror," and his worship involved the use of polished obsidian mirrors known as tezcatl. In some representations, a black mirror is shown in his chest. Aztec sorcerers would gaze into these mirrors to commune with their ancestors and gain access to the spirit world. In the 16th century, one of these mirrors made its way to England and into the possession of John Dee (1527-1608). Dee was a fascinating fellow, one of those people whose life story is both too crazy to be true but too weird to be made up. He was influential as both a mathematician and scientist, reputed to be the most learned man of his day. The line between the scientific and the mystical was even less clear-cut back in those days than it is now, and Dee served as the astrological advisor to Queen Elizabeth I, choosing the date for her coronation based on his study of the stars. It was Dee who gave us the term "The British Empire" and who first called the Americas "The New World." He is rumored to have served as a spy, and his letters in that capacity were supposedly signed using the code name 007. Despite all these extraordinary activities, it was as a magician that Dr. Dee made his most lasting reputation.

Dee was a polymath and a voracious seeker after knowledge. His personal library was said to be one of the best in Europe. He was acknowledged as an authority in mathematics, navigation, and the physical sciences. He even made his own contribution to the world of theatre when, as a student, he produced the special effects for a production of Aristophanes's *Peace*, including a mechanical scarab beetle that appeared on stage during the play's climax. The *outré* nature of these special effects gave Dee the beginning of his reputation as a sorcerer.

Dee's quest for knowledge had led him to experiment with magical techniques, including scrying, using the mirror sacred to Tezcatlipoca as a shew stone in an attempt to gain insights from the spirit world. Finding his own talents lacking, he had explored the use of mediums to engage in the activity of scrying while Dee himself acted as scribe. After failing to find success with a number of mediums, Dee made contact with Edward Kelley (1555-1598). Kelley was a man with a colorful past that included alchemy and forgery. He had the habit of wearing a skullcap to hide where his ears had been removed as punishment for these activities. Whatever Kelley's past, he appeared to have a talent for scrying. The results of the experiments were, according to Dee's account, wildly successful with contact made with angelic beings. These communications were laboriously transcribed, and through them Dee supposedly received a record of the Angelic language, also referred to as "Enochian." The records of these experiments were eventually published in

1659 by the scholar Méric Casaubon, as *A True & Faithful Relation of What Passed for many Yeers between Dr. John Dee (A Mathematician of Great Fame in Q. Eliz. and King James their Reignes) and some spirits*. Dee and Kelley's relationship ended in 1589 after some strain, caused in part by Kelley's claim that the angels had commanded for himself and Dee to engage in intercourse with each other's wives. Dee died at the age of eighty-one, out of favor with the court of King James I, his library ransacked, and his reputation destroyed.

Despite his loss of respectability and favor later in life, Dee obtained immortality in Elizabethan theatre. It is possible that Shakespeare based *The Tempest's* sorcerer Prospero on Dee, and elements of Dee's public reputation as a summoner and necromancer can be clearly seen in Christopher Marlowe's *Faust*.

Faust and The Devil's Pact

In F.W. Murnau's 1926 silent adaptation of the Faust story, we see an aged and weary Faust, desperate to end the plague that has stricken his village. He is unaware that he is the subject of a Job-like pact between Heaven and Hell, casting a circle around himself at a lonely rural crossroads with the intent to summon up the Devil. Murnau was one of the supreme visual imaginations of the German Expressionist film movement of the 1920s and '30s, and we see his signature use of strange angles and distorted visuals, used to make us feel that strangeness and danger of a trip to the Crossroads and meeting with the Devil face-to-face.

Like Robert Johnson, the story of Faust is one of those strange myths where we can point with some certainty at the actual person it was based on. Georg (or Jorg) Faust was a German magician, alchemist, and astrologer who lived in the late fifteenth and early sixteenth centuries. He appears at various points in the historical record, which records a variety of misadventures including claiming before a crowd to be able to recreate the miracles of Christ, acting as a spy and agent for Catholic bishops, threatening to curse the city of Ingolstadt, his subsequent exile from the city, and claiming to have received magical powers due to a pact with the Devil. Given the number of incidents recorded and the timespan in which they appear, ranging from the early 1500s to the 1530s, it has been suggested that there were at least two German magicians going by the name of Faust. Whether there was one historical Faust or two, we do know that the legend spread quickly, mixing with existing tales told of legendary magicians such as Simon Magus and the Polish Pan Twardowski, to create a substantial body of myth and folklore. Popular chapbooks telling his story sold briskly. The title of a 1587 edition gives us a good indication of the state of his story at the time:

> *History of Dr Johann Faustus, the Notorious Magician and Necromancer. How He Sold Himself to the Devil for an Appointed Time, What Strange Adventures He Saw in that Interval, Himself Inventing Some and Living through Others, Until He Received at Last his Well-Deserved Requital.*

These early versions of the story explicitly tie the Faustian pact to a meeting at a crossroads. In one of the first Faust books, we are told how Faust, "Toward evening, at a crossroad in these woods, he described certain circles with his staff, so that, beside twain, the two which stood above intersected a large circle. Thus in the night between nine and ten o'clock he did conjure the Devil."

In addition to books telling the story of Faust, a number of grimoires such as *Doctor Johannes Faust's Threefold Coercion of Hell* and *The Black Raven* appeared either attributed to or associated with the black magician. Their content is quite typical of other grimoires of the time, with the names and seals of demons who may be summoned, descriptions of the functions of these demons and magic circles, and names of power that may be used to command the demons. The Faust grimoires come out of the same German family of magical texts that include the Sixth and Seventh Books of Moses, which we have seen were commonly used by American hoodoo and voodoo practitioners in the nineteenth and twentieth centuries.

THE GOD OF THE CROSSROADS

The fictionalized Faust is usually accompanied by the demon Mephistopheles, who is charged with ensuring Faust sticks to the conditions of the pact. Mephistopheles acts as the Trickster, encouraging Faust to waste the powers for which he sold his soul on pranks. In Christopher Marlowe's *Tragical History of the Life and Death of Doctor Faustus*, Faust turns invisible and enters the papal court, stealing the Pope's food and later giving the Pope a blow to the face. In another incident, he causes a knight to grow horns on his head. At the end of the play, having sold his soul and wasted the power he was granted in exchange on frivolity and jests, Faust is dragged to Hell at the appointed time.

Faust is a complex figure, at once both tragic and heroic. The story, as told by Marlowe, is more than a simple morality tale and has a strong Promethean flavor. Faust has challenged the power of God in Heaven and God's representatives on Earth. He acts as a counterpart to the Biblical Job. In many tellings, Faust is, like the biblical Job, the subject of a wager between the forces of light and darkness as to whether a good man can retain his faith in the face of suffering and hardship. Later tellings, beginning with Goethe's epic retelling, often emphasize these aspects of the tale and show how Faust can obtain salvation, not through good works or faith but the power of his own inexorable will.

One of the oldest stories about making a pact with the Devil at the Crossroads is the tale of the sixth century cleric Theophilus of Adana. Theophilus was said to be a Turkish deacon who was nominated for the position of bishop. Feeling unworthy of such a high-ranking role, Theophilus turned down the offer in the expectation that the new bishop, for whom he had stepped aside, would return the favor and grant Theophilus a prominent ecclesiastical position. The offer was not forthcoming as expected and, offended by this slight, Theophilus sought the aid of a sorcerer. The sorcerer agreed to take Theophilus to a crossroads where they met with the Devil, and the cleric signs a contract in his own blood in which Theophilus renounces Christ and the Virgin Mary. In exchange, his rival was deposed and Theophilus granted the role he had previously declined. The end of the story takes a more pious turn where, after reflecting on the long-term consequences of giving up his eternal soul, Theophilus prays to the Virgin Mary who intercedes on his behalf and grants absolution, releasing Theophilus from his infernal contract.

Bridges are also favorite places of the Devil. Like crossroads, they are a liminal space, a place of crossing between. "Devil's Bridges" can be found in many places in Europe including the Pont du Diable over the Hérault River in France, the Steinerne Brücke in Regensburg, Germany, and the Devil's Bridge in Ceredigion, Wales. Various tales about the Devil are associated with these bridges. In the most common version, the Devil offers to assist the builder of the bridge in exchange for the first soul to cross the bridge. The Devil is outwitted when the cunning bridge-builder sends a dog across the bridge. Crossing the gap between one place and another, bridges are another example of a place "in-between" and can be considered a variation on the crossroads. We see in this story a typical example of the Devil as a Trickster, in this case, one where he finds himself outwitted.

During the witch hunts of the fifteenth to eighteenth centuries, witches were accused of entering into bargains with the Devil. The fifteenth century *Malleus Maleficarum* ("The Hammer of the Witches") goes into great detail about the supposed nature of this pact and how, through it, witches derive their powers. In the superstitions and hysteria that grew during the witch craze, witches were often depicted gathering together for the wild dances and orgiastic rites later termed "the witches' Sabbath." Depictions of the witches' Sabbath tell us of wild dancing to instruments such as the fiddle, which carried a reputation for impropriety since its introduction to Europe in the fifteenth century. Despite its later association with more genteel music, the fiddle was originally an instrument of the dancehall and the tavern and associated with sinfulness.

One of the most curious cases of the Devil's Pact is the case of French priest Urbain Grandier (1590-1634). Handsome and well connected, Grandier was trained by the Jesuits and in 1617 granted the position of parish priest at the Church of Saint-Pierre-du-Marche in the town of Loudon. In 1632, the nuns at the nearby convent began exhibiting unusual behavior. At first, they simply shut themselves away and refused to accept visitors. Later, their behavior became more strange and violent, including compulsive shouting, barking, and foul language. The authorities investigated the matter, and the nuns blamed their behavior on Grandier, who they accused of being a black magician who had sold his soul to the Devil. Grandier was arrested. During his trial, and under pain of torture, a document that purported to be Grandier's diabolical pact was produced, outlining the terms of the deal and featuring the signatures of Satan, Leviathan, Beelzebub, and others. Grandier was found guilty and burned at the stake on August 18, 1634.

The god of the Crossroads has often been associated with music, and the violin is a favorite instrument. The most famous modern example is Charlie Daniels's 1979 hit "The Devil Went Down to Georgia." Since its introduction from the Middle East in the fifteenth century, the violin has had an association with paganism, lust, and drinking. Witches were said to dance to fiddle music at the witches' sabbath, and the Devil himself is often depicted as a fiddle player in folktales. The Italian composer Giuseppe Tartini (1692-1770) claimed that the Devil appeared to him in a dream and played for him the piece that Tartini later published as "The Devil's Trill." The famed Italian violinist Niccolò Paganini (1782-1840) was rumored to have sold his soul to the Devil in exchange for his extraordinary proficiency with the instrument, including the virtuosic ability to play at the blinding speed of twelve notes per second. Passionate, popular, and wild, Paganini lived a life as extraordinary as his talent on his chosen instrument, a life that left him intimately familiar with the palaces of kings and the insides of prisons, the heights of culture and the depths of drug addiction. Audience members even reported seeing the Devil standing with Paganini on stage, guiding his hand. On account of these rumors, after his death, the church refused to allow Paganini's remains to be buried on church grounds. Keen-eared listeners will notice that his "Caprice No. 5" was used as the basis for the piece "Eugene's Trick Bag," played by Steve

A MEETING AT THE CROSSROADS: ROBERT JOHNSON AND THE DEVIL

Vai portraying the Devil's leather-pantsed, superstrat-shredding champion in Walter Hill's 1986 film *Crossroads*.

What Happens at the Crossroads?

So what's all this got to do with Robert Johnson? It's nice to know about this "God of the Crossroads" and pacts with the Devil and all that, but what does this tell us about the subject of this book?

The Crossroads isn't an event. It's a way of being. More than that, it's a way of becoming, of continuous transformation between states of being. The people who suppose that a quick midnight trip down to backroads Mississippi will save them years of guitar practice and earn them worldwide fame to boot, are putting the cart and the horse the wrong way around.

For some, the quest for the Crossroads is the quest for authenticity. This is perhaps what the guns of white blues guitar were chasing in the '60s. They had the chops, and in many cases, they had earned the respect and even the admiration of the blues players they were emulating. But they remained a step removed from the music. Mike Bloomfield's short book *Me and Big Joe* sums it up well. Bloomfield, having paid his dues on the Chicago club circuit and earning fame in the Paul Butterfield Blues Band, struck up a friendship with Delta bluesman Big Joe Williams, who had recorded hits that later became standards, including "Baby Please Don't Go" and "Crawling Kingsnake," for the Bluebird label in the 1930s and '40s and was at the time experiencing a career revival on the festival circuit. Bloomfield wanted to experience the blues outside of his familiar Chicago clubs, and Williams took Bloomfield to Milwaukee and St. Louis, where Bloomfield was slammed between the eyes with a world that wasn't his own. Bloomfield was taken into the heart of black America, where he encountered a world of poverty, of people living in derelict buildings with open pit latrines. As hot a guitar slinger Bloomfield was, as accepted as he was by the living masters of the genre, he still remained a step away from the real blues. The more he chased that elusive claim for authenticity, the further away it got. No wonder the instant fix seemed so tempting to some.

The Crossroads isn't the instant fix. Let's look back at Johnson. The popular version of the myth tells us that Johnson wasn't any good, that he just flailed away on the guitar and made a racket before disappearing for a short time and returning with sudden unexpected skill. This just isn't the case. By the time he was in the Delta, jamming on the scene with Son House, Willie Brown, and the like, he already had the miles under his belt. He could play music; he knew the hot sounds coming out of Memphis. But even when playing songs he knew well, if he wanted to keep a rowdy Delta crowd jumping, he needed to learn something about the local style. He needed to get the rhythm and the beat; he needed to learn to stand tall and play out those blues with authority.

Johnson had already been through some changes. His family life was anything other than stable. He'd already lost a wife and child. In a colloquial sense, that's a crossroads moment, a time of change, but it's not the moment we're looking for. He was still moving, still growing. We don't know how the loss of Virginia Travis changed Johnson, but it's clear from the accounts before and after this time that he still hadn't grown into the Robert Johnson he'd be known as the world over.

What about his apprenticeship with Ike Zimmerman? This strange relationship gave Johnson the skills he needed to impress Son House; he'd made his way from apprentice to journeyman to master bluesman, but that was still just the beginning of the journey. A formal or semi-formal apprenticeship or initiation, like Johnson went through with Zimmerman, is an important part of the story, but it's only the beginning. The true transformation, that thing we call the Crossroads, is still to come.

Let's step back and look at a fellow we met previously. Stagger Lee is the kind of man who's been to the Crossroads. There's nothing in the Stagger Lee stories, toasts or songs that tells us this outright, but it's implicit in the telling.

A MEETING AT THE CROSSROADS: ROBERT JOHNSON AND THE DEVIL

He's the man so far outside what's considered right and proper that he's become larger than life. Stagger Lee became a mythic figure before the real man had been lowered into the ground. When Johnson left Zimmerman and re-encountered House, he'd become adept at the local style, another skilled blues player and singer among many, and even if he had recorded at this stage, he would have been nothing more than another of the many lesser-known guitarists of the era, perhaps revered by collectors and aficionados but not the larger-than-life figure he was to become. He was a man, but, like Stagger Lee, he was to become something more.

The blues is a tradition. Authenticity matters; staying true to the style and the form matters. Stray too far from the form and you're no longer playing the blues. Blues becomes rock and roll, soul, R&B. An argument can be made that if you strip back the layers of contemporary EDM, you'll even find traces of the blues there. But having the roots in something is different to *being* something. The Wu Tang Clan's RZA (performing as Bobby Digital) may have used a B.B. King sample to build his 2001 track "Can't Lose." The Fat Possum label collaborated with Tom Rothrock and Lyrics Born to turn R.L. Burnside's hill country grooves into a mutant, remixed hybrid of blues, hip-hop, and electronica. Moby's Alan Lomax samples on his career-reviving album *Play*. All this acknowledges the role blues played in laying the foundations for contemporary music, but coming from a thing is different to being a thing.

Robert Johnson's music *is* the blues. When you listen to the music of Robert Johnson back-to-back with the Mississippi artists who inspired him, such as House, Patton, the Mississippi Sheiks, or Skip James, it's the differences that stand out as much as the similarities. Johnson's right hand plays a rolling boogie rhythm inspired by the blues piano player's left hand, and, while he may use floating verses, Johnson's songs are tightly arranged to fit the format of the 78 rpm record. His use of the bottleneck is precise and targeted. Johnson's transformation of the form means that the difference between his "Preaching Blues" and the House song that inspired it is as great as the difference between Cream's "Crossroads" and Johnson's "Crossroads Blues."

There's one difference though. While Cream's rendition comes from the blues, it's clearly a product of the rock and roll era. As great and innovative as it was, whatever it is, it's no longer the blues. The song is taken outside the tradition that birthed it. Johnson, however, whether he's adapting "Preaching Blues" or "Devil Got My Woman" or "Sittin' On Top of the World" or any of the many songs that he used to build his recorded repertoire, is always staying within the tradition even as he expands it in ways to create sounds that had never been heard before.

Listeners whose exposure to the Delta blues is largely limited to Robert Johnson are often surprised, even shocked, when hearing the music Johnson quoted. No effort is made to hide the source. If anything, the swipes and references are thrown out there in the open with a nod and a knowing wink. We're *supposed* to recognize them. The refrain of "Sweet Home Chicago" directly quotes Scrapper Blackwell's "Kokomo Blues," right down to the cry, "baby don't you wanna go." "Walkin' Blues" has clear roots in the music of Son House, "32-20 Blues" is derived from Skip James's "22-20 Blues," and so on. The blues tradition has always worked in this manner. We've already seen how motifs, such as road and railway crossings, get picked up and repeated with variation throughout the tradition. When Junior Wells called his 1965 Delmark release *Hoodoo Man Blues*, we're supposed to pick up the reference to John Lee "Sonny Boy" Williamson's "Hoodoo Hoodoo." Willie Dixon's "Little Red Rooster" draws from Charley Patton's "Banty Rooster." That's the way music like this works. You take what's gone before, you add something new, and you cast it out into the world, expanding on the tradition, creating new possibilities for those who are still to come. Listeners who only know what you've done without knowing what's gone before are missing half the story. The act of creating and performing this music is an act of simultaneously building on what's gone before and making something new that's never been heard before. New suits, old cloth.

On repeated listening, it's not the similarities that stand out so much as the differences. While Scrapper Blackwell was best known for his work with pianist Leroy Carr, "Kokomo Blues" was recorded as a solo piece. In Johnson's adaptation, he adds the missing piano accompaniment, imitating the back-and-forth rhythm lines on the bass strings of his guitar. Crucially, Johnson's recordings are a product of the recorded age. His tutelage under Zimmerman and his ramblings with Edwards, Shines, and the rest taught him to play the blues successfully before a crowd. Johnson took this and found a new way to play the Delta blues before a crowd he couldn't see.

Robert Johnson's repertoire was wider than the blues. Johnny Shines and Honeyboy Edwards both tell us that he could perform country, pop, or whatever was required to bring in the tips when playing on the street. It's possible to hear traces of these genres in Johnson's recordings—Johnson's plaintive howls and moans can be more than a little reminiscent of Jimmie Rodgers's "Blue Yodels"—but there's no indication that he was in any way innovative in his approach to these genres. Shines has described Johnson as a human jukebox who could hear a song just once and then bash out a rendition to fulfill a request or give the crowd what it needed. He could play those songs, but there's nothing that says his renditions were notable or innovative. He knew the songs and the music, he played it well, but that's about it. But his blues—that was something else. We've seen how jealously he guarded his techniques. It may even have been Johnny Temple using his boogie rhythms on "Lead Pencil Blues" that finally convinced Johnson to head on down to H.C. Spier's for an audition. Johnson was doing something new, and he damn well knew it. He was taking the tradition, making it into something new without changing what it was. Like the caterpillar that already contains the essence of the butterfly it will become, or the larvae of the dung beetle emerge from their ball of shit already carrying within them the imprint of the grown beetle, Johnson took the Delta blues he was playing and made it more itself, marrying it with other styles he heard growing up in Memphis and on his travels and used it to make a new form entirely his own. This was recognized even in his own time. That's why the white record collectors were so keen to hear his music even while he was still alive, why he was booked for the From Spirituals to Swing concert, why Muddy Waters cited him as a major influence even if in all probability he never saw Johnson play, why Shines, Edwards, and Lockwood kept on championing his music even if they grew to bristle at any mention of the Devil. The music was that good, it was something that hadn't been heard before, and in itself, he contained the blueprint of the music that was to come. Not just rock and roll, as the auto-hagiographies of the Baby Boomer generation would have it, but the electric, urban blues of Chicago, the stripped-back sounds of the West Side Chicago style, the blending of Delta and jump blues we hear in B.B. King, the soul of Albert King, Little Milton, and Bobby "Blue" Bland, and on it goes. Johnson sits at the center, acting as a kind of Rosetta Stone, allowing us to understand the early blues in the context of what came after and vice versa. Johnson isn't held up as the King of the Delta Blues just because he's the guy that was rediscovered and championed; he was rediscovered and championed because his music is that damn good and that damn important.

And this is what the Crossroads is all about and why the story got attached so strongly to Johnson, even if he wasn't the first to do it, even if we can't be certain it was explicitly attached to Johnson during his lifetime. This is what the god of the Crossroads does. He seeks after new knowledge, takes what was there before, and transforms it to become not a new thing but the thing it always could be. Hermes, Seth, Odin, Legba and all the others we explored, their function is always to transform things from one state of being to another. This isn't always easy, which is why this transformation is often explained in violent terms like the slaying of Osiris or Odin's self-sacrifice. Johnson was a transformer, a changer, an innovator. And he had a song about the Crossroads. The story about a midnight pact at the Crossroads practically writes itself.

When did Johnson make this transition from interpreting the music to changing it from the inside? It can only be some time in Johnson's rambling years, after his encounter with House and before his audition for H.C. Spier. Making his living as a walking musician, Johnson absorbed the influences around him and was forced to prove himself or starve. Johnson wasn't the first musician to rely on the graces of the public to earn his meal ticket, and he won't be the last. A quick trip down Bourbon Street in New Orleans or Sixth Street in Austin is enough to confirm that for a fact. But he took the opportunity to learn from everyone that he met and used it to build a style and repertoire that was uniquely his own. He mastered the form, internalized it, and from this produced something entirely new.

This is the state of being that we call the Crossroads. It's an ongoing experience of work and transformation. It's a state of being outside what *is* because you can see what *is to be*. This is why the Crossroads is the work of the Devil. It is an essentially antinomian state that exists outside of current works and frames of reference. It is not always a successful quest. A quick browse through the history of artists who came up short of something new is enough to confirm that, and it can be a dangerous one. Check back on that list of artists you just made in your head and check the ages of death if you want to confirm that one for yourself.

As we've seen, the idea of the bluesman making a deal at the Crossroads wasn't unique to Robert Johnson. In various forms, whether made at the fork of two or three roads or in a graveyard, whether the deal was made at midnight or dawn, whether the deal was for skill with guitar or luck with the dice, the deal with the Devil was an existing part of blues lore well before it became associated with Johnson. Digging into the stories, one sees the event is always vague and nebulous. You're not going to get a signed and dated contract. It's not a thing that happened at a time or a place. It's a reflection on the nature of the bluesman. By living a life outside norms, at the center of the juking, drinking, and gambling life that respectable folks are supposed to reject, the story of the Crossroads is used to describe folk who are of the Devil's party through their rejection of everything upright folks are supposed to be.

As the god of the Outsider, the god of the Crossroads is associated with these types. In ancient times, foreigners were as much those who did not adhere to accepted cultural taboos as they were people from a foreign country. The pushing, questioning, and breaking of taboos was a task sacred to all Tricksters. This is the process through which change and transformation takes place.

This, then, is the final secret of the Crossroads. Johnson was a transformer, a man who mastered a form and then used it to create something new. In doing this, he was participating in an archetype that was older than he could know. As a bluesman, he was an outsider, a man who stood apart from the community around him, who turned his back on the faith, a man who walked the same path as Stagolee and Peetie Wheatstraw. As he transformed the music he played, he was walking side-by-side with the Devil, with the god of the Crossroads, preparing the way for further changes to come. People are right to say that the Crossroads is the place where you meet the Devil, but you won't find them in Clarksdale, Rosedale, or Rolling Fork. The Crossroads is the place where you change yourself and where, through this change, you transform the world.

[1] Aeneid, Book IV, 511
   [2] Hyde, 1998, p173
   [3] Hyde, 1998, p10
   [4] Gussow, 2017, p12
   [5] Matthew 16:19

Conclusion

For a music that hews so closely to tradition, the blues doesn't stand still. Go to a Southern juke today, especially if you go outside of tourist season, and you'll hear a modern sound full of drum machines, synths, and aggressively auto-tuned vocals shaped as much by Kanye West as by Robert Johnson or B.B. King. It's still blues, just blues that evolved along a different, more soulful path. Every now and then, the white blues collectors' dream of uncovering a backwoods bluesman comes true, but oftentimes, they'll wear their overalls when playing for the blues collectors and their high-style suit when performing for their home crowd.

This transformation is what the Crossroads is all about. It's about a music and a tradition moving forward while still maintaining its essence. This is what Robert Johnson did when he took the sounds he learned growing up in Memphis, as well the broader American sounds he heard in his ramblings, and used them to create his own style of Delta blues and then distilled it down to an essence that could be captured on a single side of a 78 rpm record.

The Crossroads is an ancient symbol of change. The god of the Crossroads rules over initiation, transformation, moving from one state to another. He is the god of the outsider, of those who move out of step with those around them.

Even by the standards of the bluesman, Johnson lived a life apart. He presented different faces to different people. The stories told by Son House, Honeyboy Edwards, Robert Lockwood Jr., and Annye C. Anderson tell us of a man who could be aloof and mean but also tender and caring and who, above all else, was consumed by his music. In the end, it was the lifestyle associated with his music that killed him, but it is also his music that lives on. Going back and listening to Johnson's tunes, it can be surprising how *modern* they sound. Johnson was pushing forward, hearing sounds in his head that nobody had heard before. The music transformed him, and by being captured on record, the music went out and transformed the world. Robert Johnson lives on; you can find him on dusty dorm room record players, in run-down recording studios, dive-bar jam sessions, on film, on record, anywhere where people discover his story and are inspired into an act of creation. I told you at the beginning that the story of the Crossroads was a lie. I confess that I was telling a little white lie myself. Robert Johnson met the Devil at the Crossroads when he chose to not just live the life of a bluesman, but when he used this life to create a music that nobody had ever heard before. He may not have sold his soul, but he was a true poet and of the Devil's party. The god of the Crossroads knows his own.

APPENDIX A: Discovering the Crossroads

If you want to fully understand the Crossroads, you have to go to the land where the blues began. Even if you're a seasoned traveler to the United States, or live there yourself, the rural South can feel like a totally different country. It has its own beliefs and customs, a shared history through good and bad that makes it unlike anywhere else on the planet. You'll find the blues there, both literally and metaphorically, both in terms of the music in a form that's a million miles from the sanitized version used to sell light beer, and in the emotional sense. Wounds cut in the days of the Civil Rights battle, even the Civil War, are still open, waiting to be healed. Be advised that a quest for the Crossroads can often lead you to your own personal crossroads encounter. When you visit the land of the blues, a small part of it will stay with you forever. The blues is still a living, evolving tradition and the emphasis here is places where you can encounter this tradition as it stands today. Memorials of time gone by can teach you so much. Juking it up on a Saturday in Mississippi - That's where you'll really find the Crossroads.

Note that, at the time of writing, Mississippi and the rest of the South are still suffering from the impact of the COVID-19 pandemic. Visitors are certainly welcome, but when traveling, stay sensible, stay safe, and pay attention to any safety, distancing, or masking directions.

LOOKING FOR THE CROSSROADS

APPENDIX A: DISCOVERING THE CROSSROADS

For those of you who've skipped straight to the back of the book looking for the good stuff, I'm sorry to say that I can't tell you the location of the "real crossroads" any more than I can take you to Shangri-La, Lilliput, or the Miskatonic University. What I *can* do is list some places that are part of the Crossroads story. They're all places where one road crosses another, and they all form a link in the chain of the story of Robert Johnson and the blues.

The Clarksdale Crossroads Monument

This is the famous one, at the intersection of Highways 61 and 49, the monument that you'll find on the postcards and t-shirts. The location was known as "The Crossroads" long before any association with Johnson for the simple reason that it's a major four-way intersection on the way in and out of town. While any genuine link to Johnson's story is dubious at best, it's still a bucket-list item for many people, and this has created a genuine sense of magic and mystery about the place, even if the sign itself is a little small and located on a traffic island in between two major highways. Pop by, get your photo op, post it on Instagram, then go across the road to Abe's for some proper BBQ.

Corner State Street and Desoto Ave, Clarksdale, Mississippi

The Other Clarksdale Crossroads

A number of perceptive folk have pointed out that while the Crossroads monument is located on the intersection of the mythical Highways 61 and 49, this location reflects the modern placement of the roads, and the particular highways didn't cross at that point back in Johnson's day. The former crossing of these two highways is located closer to the center of town, near the intersection of West Tallahatchie Street and Martin Luther King Boulevard. In Johnson's time, this part of town was the center of Clarksdale's African American nightlife, where he would have performed and gambled and drank. It fits the theme, although with nightlife sometimes peaking in the small hours of the morning, it is difficult to see how a midnight rendezvous with Mephistopheles could have been arranged. There's not much to see there nowadays, although it falls conveniently on the way between the famous Crossroads monument and Red's Juke Joint.

324 Martin Luther King Blvd., Clarksdale, Mississippi

Dockery Plantation

Located forty miles out of Clarksdale, Dockery Plantation may be the place with the strongest claim as the birthplace of the Delta Blues. Musicians known to have either worked on or performed at the plantation form a genuine *Who's Who* of the Delta blues, including Howlin' Wolf, Son House, Charley Patton, and, of course, Robert Johnson. The location itself is fairly basic. Some buildings from the era are still standing; there is a Blues Trail Marker providing some basic history of the plantation and its significance to the blues, and there's a button you can press to hear a few brief snatches of Charley Patton's music, a cheap trick, perhaps, but spine-chilling all the same. Still, make no mistake, this *is* sacred ground, the equivalent for the dedicated blues fan of visiting Jerusalem or Mecca. As an added bonus, the area is surrounded by a number of rural roads that all meet together *just so*. Tour operators have claimed any number of them as *the* Crossroads. They certainly look the part. Maybe you'll have to visit them at midnight just to make sure…

229 Highway 8, Cleveland, Mississippi
www.dockeryfarms.org
Ph 662-719-1048

Rosedale

In "Traveling Riverside Blues," Johnson sang about going down to Rosedale.

The British supergroup Cream added this verse to their 1968, hard-rock interpretation of "Crossroads." Since then, the story has grown that Rosedale, Mississippi, population 1800, forty miles south of Clarksdale, is the site of the real Crossroads. The locals certainly don't do their part to dispel the legend, naming the now defunct local blues association the Crossroads Blues Society and with a Mississippi Blues Trail marker sitting dutifully at the intersection of Highways 1 and 8. Pop on by; Rosedale is a good town, if suffering from the loss of downtown all-American small towns are going through, but without the blues revival money they have in Clarksdale.

Highways 1 and 8, Rosedale, Mississippi
(Set your GPS to N33° 51.103' W91° 01.496')

The above are the main locations, but there are others. I've heard rumors about a spot just outside of Clarksdale on the way to the Shack Up Inn, and another 100 miles north of Clarksdale, where Highways 61 and 49 meet just outside a graveyard. If you ask around, you'll get any number of suggestions. Take them with a grain of salt and remember, it's not the place that matters, it's the state of being.

THE MANY GRAVES OF ROBERT JOHNSON

It is appropriate for Johnson, a figure who has reached mythical status, to have multiple resting places, just like the Egyptian god Osiris, whose multiple graves and cult centers were explained by his body being cut into fourteen pieces, or the Christian saints and martyrs with their plurality of relics and places of pilgrimage. Even Jesus Christ himself has both the Church of the Holy Sepulchre and the Garden Tomb competing for the title of his burial place. Fortunately for the modern-day blues pilgrim, the purported graves and memorials are all relatively close to one another and can be easily visited in a single day.

Payne Chapel Missionary Baptist Church

A small memorial was placed here in 1990 by members of the obscure Atlanta rock band the Tombstones. The story goes that they read an article in *Living Blues* citing this as a possible location and decided to pool their funds and right a wrong by giving Johnson a proper memorial. While the site is lacking in the way of provenance, it is still significant as the first memorial for Johnson raised at a proper burial site. The location isn't well signposted, so you'll have to rely on your GPS to find it and the grave itself will take a little hunting to find. If you're having trouble finding the right spot, look for your fellow blues travelers; there always seems to be a few of them hanging about.

32830 County Road 167, Itta Bena, Mississippi
(Set your GPS to 33.4408, -90.3036)

Mt. Zion Missionary Baptist Church

On April 29, 1991, a second memorial was erected, this one located a little down the road near Morgan City. This one was erected with the assistance of ZZ Top, no doubt still doing a little better than your typical garage rockers after selling over 10 million copies of *Eliminator*, and Columbia Records, doing well after the unexpected success of *The Complete Recordings*, and the stone is correspondingly a little more elaborate than the one down the road, engraved with the titles of Johnson's recorded songs, song lyrics, and a brief biography. The official story is that this is not intended to be a gravestone marking the actual resting place, but rather a memorial. The story doesn't prevent people from leaving offerings of booze, money, and guitar picks in front of the memorial stone.

Phillipston Rd, (County Road 511), Morgan City, Mississippi
(Set your GPS to 33.3919, -90.3102)

Little Zion Missionary Baptist Church

This is the one that actually stands a chance of being the real deal. Based on the testimony of Johnson's half sister and the wife of the grave digger, the stone stands either on or near the spot where Johnson may actually be buried. Unfortunately, the stone itself is decorated with a facsimile of an almost certainly fraudulent deathbed confession in which Johnson supposedly renounces his devilish ways and commends his soul to the Lord. I suppose the Devil doesn't mind a little white lie here and there.

Money Road, Greenwood, Mississippi
(Set your GPS to 33.5638 - 90.2159)

CLARKSDALE

If any city can claim to be "ground zero" of the blues, then it has got to be Clarksdale. Just about every major figure in Mississippi and Chicago blues lived here or played here or passed on through. Clarksdale was the last stopping point before making your way to Memphis, a literal crossroads where major transport routes meet before heading north. Over the years, the town has experienced both good times and bad, including, over the past twenty years, a tourist revival fed by the blues. The recent pandemic has slowed things somewhat, but the blues is a resilient thing and you can't keep it down for long.

Cat Head Delta Blues and Folk Art

Located on Delta Avenue in the heart of downtown, Cat Head is the first place anyone visiting Clarksdale should call. Owner Roger Stolle (ably assisted by blues pug Miss Ayler) keeps his finger on the pulse and knows everything blues-related that's going on in town. His weekly "Sounds Around Town" updates give you a guide to live gigs, and he'll happily point you in the direction of anything blues-based, or otherwise, that you might need. Just don't forget to pick up a book, CD, poster, or baseball cap while you're there.

A MEETING AT THE CROSSROADS: ROBERT JOHNSON AND THE DEVIL

252 Delta Ave, Clarksdale, Mississippi
www.cathead.biz
Ph 662-624-5992

Red's Lounge

"Backed by the river, fronted by the grave," Red's is everything you want in a Mississippi juke joint. Dimly lit and dripping with atmosphere, you can catch genuine live blues here up to four nights a week, more during festival season. Owner Red Paden runs a tight ship. The place might look rough, but you're as safe as if you were in your own living room. Grab yourself a bottle of Bud and kick back with local blues from the likes of Big A and the Allstars, Deak Harp, Lucious Spiller, and more. Be sure to come by early if you're visiting when there's a festival going on, as the place can fill up early in the night. If you're visiting at other times of the year, you might find you have the joint pretty much to yourself. Both ways are fine by me, and they each, in their own way, give you an authentic juke joint experience.

398 Sunflower Ave, Clarksdale, Mississippi
Ph 662-627-3166

Ground Zero Blues Club

A collaboration between film star Morgan Freeman and former Clarksdale mayor, the late Bill Luckett, Ground Zero Blues Club was built with one goal in mind: to provide a place where visitors can regularly find local blues in the heart of the Delta. It fulfills that goal and then some. Start the night with some burgers or a plate of catfish, fill up your glass, and be prepared to dance the night away. The venue also hosts regular blues jams for those who want to enjoy the unique experience of playing the blues at the home of the Crossroads. The place is covered with graffiti from decades of visitors, so don't forget to borrow a pen and leave your own mark on the wall. Accommodation is available upstairs for those who want a short stumble home.

387 Delta Ave, Clarksdale, Mississippi
www.groundzerobluesclub.com
Ph 662-621-9009

Bad Apple Blues Club

The newest of the Mississippi jukes, located on the site of the former Club 2000, the Bad Apple Blues Club is the home of Mississippi and Memphis blues veteran Sean "Bad" Apple. You'll catch Sean performing here when he isn't booked elsewhere, and you can expect him to always give it his all and deliver a genuine Mississippi blues party, whether he's playing to two people or 200.

349 Issaquena Ave, Clarksdale, Mississippi
www.facebook.com/badappleblucsclub/

The Delta Blues Museum

This is about as close as Clarksdale gets to a conventional tourist attraction. Travel through the history of the blues from the plantations to the modern day. Discover artifacts such as Muddy Waters's cabin and more guitars than you can poke a stick at. Bonus points to the curators for going beyond merely displaying artifacts and taking the time to tell the story of the blues as experienced by the people who lived it. An absolutely essential visit, and one of the best museums around, but lacking the quirkiness and Southern charm you'll find elsewhere in town. The museum regularly hosts special events during the festival season.

1 Blues Alley, Clarksdale, Mississippi
www.deltabluesmuseum.org
Ph 662-627-6820

The Shack Up Inn

It's a few miles out of town, but if you have a car this is one of the best damn accommodation experiences you can have while road-tripping the South. Their slogan might declare "The Ritz we ain't," but these refurbished sharecropper shacks offer a better night's sleep than you'll find at any Holiday Inn, with 1,000 times the atmosphere. Each shack can sleep two to four guests, and there's also the option of rooms in the nearby Cotton Gin Inn. As an added bonus, the on-site Juke Joint Chapel offers live music on weekends and during festival time.

1 Commissary Cir Rd, Clarksdale
www.shackupinn.com
Ph 662-624-8329

The Riverside Hotel

As authentic as it gets, the Riverside building was originally a hospital—the same one where Bessie Smith died—which became a hotel and boarding house where any famous bluesman you care to name lived or stayed when they passed through the Delta. John Lee Hooker, Howlin' Wolf, Muddy Waters, Sonny Boy Williamson—they all spent extended periods of time here. This is the place where "Rocket 88," by most accounts the first rock and roll song ever recorded, was hashed out by Ike Turner and his Kings of Rhythm before making their way to Memphis to record at Sun Studios. Facilities are basic—shared bathrooms, for example—but this is more than made up for by the sense of history and the warm hospitality from your host Zee.

615 Sunflower Ave, Clarksdale, Mississippi
www.riversideclarksdale.com
Ph 662-624-9163

LELAND

The Highway 61 Blues Museum

Off the beaten path but well worth a visit, the Highway 61 Blues Museum is a somewhat haphazardly arranged collection of various artifacts, personal effects, and musical instruments that tell the story of the blues from the inside. If you're lucky, local blues musician, folk artist, and gravedigger Pat Thomas (himself the son of bluesman Son Thomas) will wander on by and give you an impromptu performance. Be sure to check out the murals on the nearby buildings. Leland was also the childhood home of albino blues rockers Johnny and Edgar Winter and was made famous by the song "Leland Mississippi Blues" from Johnny's self-titled debut album.

307 N Broad St, Leland, Mississippi
www.highway61blues.com
Ph 662-686-7646

INDIANOLA

B.B. King Museum & Delta Interpretive Center

B.B. King lived the life that Robert Johnson was denied, going from the plantation to playing the world's largest stages. The museum takes you through the journey of his life and through it the story of the blues. For those who want to pay their respects, B.B.'s body is interred on the grounds, back home in the Delta soil.

400 2nd St, Indianola, Mississippi
www.bbkingmuseum.org
Ph 662-887-9539

Club Ebony

One of the most significant Delta jukes, Club Ebony has played host to the likes of Bobby "Blue" Bland, Ray Charles, Count Basie, and more, including, of course, B.B. King, who purchased the club in 2006. Worth going past as part of your trip to Indianola, but be advised that opening hours can be unpredictable. At the time of writing, their Facebook page is the most reliable guide to when the venue will be open and who will be performing. Specializes in Southern soul food and Southern soul blues in the tradition of Bobby "Blue" Bland and Denise LaSalle.

404 Hanna Ave, Indianola, Mississippi
www.facebook.com/pg/bbkingsclubebony/
Ph 662-887-9539

BENTONIA

A twenty-minute drive out of Yazoo City, Bentonia, a sleepy little town of only 500 or so, is the home not only of Mississippi's oldest continuously operating juke joint, but its own school of country blues. For years, blues scholars debated if the eerie, minor-key guitar style of Skip James represented the fruits of a purely personal genius or was representative of a local tradition. While the genius of James is in no doubt with the wider availability of music from other Bentonia artists such as Jack Owens and Jimmy "Duck" Holmes, the existence of a local school of blues is no longer in doubt. Skip's style of tuning the guitar to an open minor chord can be traced to his teacher Henry Stuckey, who himself claimed to have learned the tuning from Bahamian soldiers while serving in the First World War.

Whenever he's not on tour, "Duck" Holmes can usually be found inside the Blue Front Café, opened by his parents Mary and Carey Holmes in 1948. He will be happy to sell you a beer and play you some tunes. Live music features some Friday and Saturday nights. For the full Bentonia blues experience, be sure to visit the town during the annual Bentonia Blues Festival, held each year on her third Saturday in June.

Blue Front Café

The oldest continuously operating juke joint still around. Music is irregular—if you want to be certain you'll see a band, it's best to visit during the Bentonia Blues Festival. But Jimmy will be happy to play for you if he's not on tour.

107 W Railroad Ave, Bentonia, Mississippi
www.bentoniablues.com

MEMPHIS, TENNESSEE

Memphis was Johnson's first real stable home and the place where he first got to know the blues up close. It's a melting pot and a meeting point, a place to pass through and stay in when making the trip from the South to the North, or the other way around. It's a place that you've got to get to know if you're going to have any understanding of Johnson's story. While you're there, you're sure to encounter not just blues but country, hip-hop, soul, rockabilly, indie rock, and more. Genres have a way of running up against each other in Memphis. Pay attention and you might just discover something new being formed.

B.B. King's

Look, you're going to go here anyway, no matter what I tell you, and it's something you've got to do if you want to say you've been to Beale Street, but this is a straight-ahead tourist joint and proud of it. The food's good, the drink prices are reasonable, and the bands are more than solid. My advice is to check the schedule. While the primetime acts tend to focus on crowd-pleasing pop and soul acts, more straight-ahead blues acts will often be featured at other times.

143 Beale St., Memphis, Tennessee
901-524-5464
www.bbkings.com/memphis/

A. Schwab's Dry Goods

Established in 1876 and housed in one of the few remaining original buildings on Beale, A. Schwab's motto is "If you can't find it at A. Schwab, you're probably better off without it!" And they might just be right. Plenty of souvenirs, for sure, but also dry goods, a good selection of records, hoodoo and voodoo products for the casual visitor, as well as a select range of related material for the more serious practitioner. Always changing, always worth a look.

163 Beale St., Memphis, Tennessee
901-523-9782
www.a-schwab.com

Rum Boogie Café

Reliable music and BBQ joint with a strong blues focus. Acts like Vince Johnson's Plantation All-Stars and the Eric Hughs Band keep the party authentic, and the BBQ hits the spot just right. Explore the room for an impressive range of memorabilia, including the original Stax neon signs and more autographed guitars than you can poke a stick at.

182 Beale St, Memphis, Tennessee
Ph 901-528-0150
www.rumboogie.com

Mr. Handy's Blues Hall

A little brother to Rum Boogie, Mr Handy's is the closest you'll get to a juke joint feel on Beale, both the music and the decor. The room can get packed, and the party can get a little rowdy but always with a friendly vibe.

182 Beale St., Memphis, Tennessee
Ph 901-528-0150
www.rumboogie.com

Blues City Café Band Box

Attached to the restaurant next door, it's easy to walk past this little music venue without noticing that it's there. Your loss if you do: This jumping little joint provides regular work for old-school Memphis bluesmen such as Earl "The Pearl" Banks and Blind Mississippi Morris, as well as hosting showcases paying tribute to Memphis's blues, country, and rockabilly heritage.

138 Beale St., Memphis, Tennessee
Ph 901-526-3637
www.bluescitycafe.com/music/

OTHER PLACES IN MEMPHIS

Earnestine and Hazel's

Having been used as a set for films such as *Mystery Train*, *Black Snake Moan*, and *21 Grams*, you probably know what the inside of this place looks like even if you've never been there. Earnestine and Hazel's is a former brothel, almost certainly haunted, has the best damn jukebox I've ever had the pleasure of putting a dollar in, and the Soul Burger is one of the best damn burgers you'll ever have. Music is occasional, but the authentic dive-bar feel is eternal. The place seems to go in and out of fashion. I've been there when every hipster and college kid in town wanted to hang out there, I've been there when it's nearly empty on a Saturday night, and I like it fine both ways. This is one of those bars that everyone has to visit at least once in their life.

531 S Main St., Memphis, Tennessee
Ph 901-523-9754
www.earnestineandhazel.com

Wild Bill's

An absolute must if you're looking for the authentic Memphis blues, Wild Bill's is to Memphis what Red's is to Clarksdale. A genuine urban juke joint with a cooking band, great food, and a party that goes until late, this is the real Memphis experience that the other places can only pretend to be.

1580 Vollintine Ave., Memphis, Tennessee
Ph 901-409-0081
www.wildbillsmemphis.com

Sun Studios

Sacred ground. This is the place the blues met hillbilly, met R&B, met the blues to create not only the strange musical hybrid known as rock 'n' roll but also to create some astonishing music that would be guaranteed to survive until judgment day and beyond, even without the association with a man called Elvis. The tour guides know their stuff, and hearing B.B., Howlin' Wolf, The Killer, and The King come out of the speakers in the building where they recorded is guaranteed to send chills up your spine.

706 Union Avenue, Memphis, Tennessee
Ph 901- 521-0664
www.sunstudio.com

Stax Museum of American Soul Music

Although best known for its soul releases, Stax is in its own way as important to the history of the blues as Chess or Sun. Albert King, Little Milton, Little

Sonny, and others all made a lasting imprint on the blues through their sessions down on McLemore Avenue. After years of neglect, the studio has been lovingly recreated and restored while the museum helps you understand the important role the music of Stax has played in the social history of Memphis.

926 E. McLemore Ave., Memphis, Tennessee
Ph 901-261-6338
www.staxmuseum.com

Graceland

You might push back, thinking you're too cool for the American Mecca, but if you visit Memphis, you're going to find yourself visiting Graceland, no matter how hard you try to resist its call. And you know what? It's totally worth it. Just like dogs look like their owners, Graceland matches Elvis in ways that go beyond the norm. The house reflected the man, from the ostentatious kitsch of the Jungle Room to the surprisingly humble kitchens to the King's personal shooting range. The gift shops are endless, but it all forms part of the glorious contradiction of the guy who came from nothing and wound up the most famous man in the world, who could command the audience of the President of the United States, and who pottered around the house making his own midnight snacks. Elvis was immersed in Memphis' music history, an aficionado of rhythm and blues records in the days when that took genuine effort and exploring his story shines light on many aspects of Robert Johnson.

3717 Elvis Presley Blvd., Memphis, Tennessee
www.graceland.com

National Civil Rights Museum

Housed in the Lorraine Motel, where Martin Luther King Jr. was assassinated, the Civil Rights Museum is a tribute not just to Dr. King but to all who have taken part in the struggle, from the emancipation movement to the present day. Stark, confronting, and absolutely essential. You can't understand Memphis or the blues until you understand the story told here.

450 Mulberry St., Memphis, TN
Ph 901-521-9699
www.civilrightsmuseum.org

APPENDIX B: A Listener's Guide to Robert Johnson

If you want to know Robert Johnson, you need to know the music. Unfortunately, the record racks and Spotify playlists can groan under the weight of unauthorized reissues with poor sound quality, inaccurately labeled compilations, and "tributes" without the talent to pull it off or the insight to know better. This brief guide is intended to help you sort the wheat from the chaff and hear Robert along with the people who he influenced, as well as the people who influenced him at their very best.

Robert Johnson, *The Centennial Collection*

The most recent, most complete edition of Johnson's recordings featuring an alternate version of "Traveling Riverside Blues" not included in previous collections. A surprise bonus is the inclusion of recording test grooves, featuring Robert's guitar noodling and speaking voice. Careful selection of sources and a sprinkling of audio wizardry means this is the best-sounding collection of his music available. Essential.

Robert Johnson, *King of the Delta Blues Singers*

If you've already got the *Centennial Collection*, why would you want this as well? Because this is how Johnson was discovered in the '60s, when he made the leap from an obscure figure whose music was only for aficionados to a major cult artist. Everything contributes to the mystique, from the faceless cover art to the liner notes to the song selection heavy with diabolic song titles. Keep in mind that for years this album represented the sum total of most blues lovers' knowledge of Robert Johnson, and all the layers of conjecture and rumor start to make sense. Be sure to get it on vinyl for the most authentic listening experience.

Charley Patton, *Rough Guide to Charley Patton*

A two-disc introduction to the work of one of the first stars of Delta blues, from the deep Delta sounds of "Pony Blues" to the polyrhythmic complexity of "Screamin' and Hollerin' the Blues" and gospel tunes like "Jesus Is a Dyin' Bed Maker." The sound quality on this collection is excellent given the source material, but it can still be a challenge for modern ears. Persistence is rewarded with not just some of the finest blues ever recorded but with new insights on every listen. Sets of Patton's complete recordings are available for those who want more, but start here first.

Standout Track: "High Water Everywhere Parts 1 & 2"

Muddy Waters, *The Complete Plantation Recordings*

Muddy's complete 1941 and 1942 recordings, made with Alan Lomax. Essential not just for the opportunity to hear one of the undisputed greats before he was famous but to see the links of the music chain take you right back to the birth of the blues. Waters specifically cited both Johnson and Son House as influences and on this recording performed with Henry "Son" Simms, who had previously performed and recorded with Son House and Charley Patton.

Standout Track: "I Be's Troubled," later electrified as Muddy's first big hit, "I Can't Be Satisfied."

Various Artists, *Roots of Robert Johnson*

APPENDIX B: A LISTENER'S GUIDE TO ROBERT JOHNSON

A single-disc guide to the artists who influenced and inspired Johnson. Important for understanding Johnson in context, not only to see what he took from his influences but also his points of departure. On Skip James's "22-20 Blues" and "Devil Got My Woman," we can hear the source of Robert's eerie falsetto, as well as the roots of one of his most popular songs, while on Scrapper Blackwell's "Kokomo Blues" we can hear the guitar boogie shuffle that became "Sweet Home Chicago."

Standout Track: The otherworldly, minor-key drone of Skip James's "Devil Got My Woman."

Son House, *The Father of the Delta Blues*

The complete post-rediscovery studio recordings of one of Robert Johnson's key inspirations. Recommended over the pre-war recordings thanks to the improved sound quality and the extra fire-in-the-belly that comes from a late-life rediscovery. House howls, moans, preaches, and beats his metal guitar like a demon from hell. Water straight from the well.

Standout Track: "Preachin' Blues" display of both defiance and fear of life in the bosom of the church.

Johnny Shines, *Johnny Shines*

Johnson's occasional traveling partner, Johnny Shines, had a rough start in the record industry, with early recordings for Columbia and Chess being deemed uncommercial and left unreleased and his J.O.B. sides failing to make a dent on the commercial market. By the mid-'60s, he had given up on music until a chance encounter with Vanguard Records led to him being recorded with a full band on volume three of *Chicago/The Blues/Today!*. He continued to record throughout the '70s in both solo and full band formats. This 1970 outing combines both, giving a possible glimpse of what Johnson would have sounded like if he had survived into the electric blues era.

Standout Track: Otis Rush's classic "I Can't Quit You Pretty Baby" is given an epic, droning makeover as "My Love Can't Hide."

Honeyboy Edwards, *Shake 'Em On Down*

This 1999 session from another of Johnson's traveling partners is astonishing for the range of material covered. Tunes derived from Charley Patton ("High Water Everywhere" and "Pony Blues"), Bukka White ("Shake 'Em on Down"), and others mix with Edward's own compositions to give a broad survey of the diversity and range of the acoustic blues tradition. Edwards's sessions could sometimes be hit and miss, but this one is pure gold from start to finish.
   Standout Track: "Anna Lee"

Robert Lockwood Jr., *Plays Robert and Robert*

A gorgeous set of solo recordings from the early '80s, featuring Robert performing tunes learned from his mentor, as well as revisiting tunes from his own illustrious career. The arrangements are updated and adapted for Lockwood's preferred twelve-string guitar, but this is in many ways a more faithful rendering of the tunes than any note-for-note renditions.

Standout Track: "Little Queen of Spades," where Lockwood mixes up the Delta style with phrasing that is pure golden-age Chicago blues.

Various Artists, *Hellhound On My Trail: Songs of Robert Johnson*

Tribute albums can be hit or miss affairs, largely depending on what artists are selected to appear. This one gets the selection right with a wide range of respected blues artists who really know their stuff including two—Honeyboy Edwards and Robert Lockwood Jr.— who actually knew and played with Robert. Add in the likes of Chris Thomas King, "Steady Rollin'" Bob Margolin and Pinetop Perkins and you've got as good a tribute album as you could hope for.

Standout Track: Honeyboy Edwards showing us how the oft-covered "Travelin' Riverside Blues" is supposed to be played.

Hayes McMullan, *Everyday Seem Like Murder Here*

In 1967, blues researcher Gayle Dean Wardlow was making his way through Mississippi, looking for old blues records. In a grocery store in Sumner, he asked a local if he had any records by the likes of Blind Lemon Jefferson or Charley Patton. The man, Hayes McMullan, replied that he didn't have any records by Charley Patton, but he used to know the man and play music with him. While he hadn't played guitar in some thirty years, McMullan was eventually persuaded to enter the studio and record some of his old reportorial as well as his spoken recollections of his time playing with Patton. The resulting document is perhaps the closest we can get to what the music sounded like in the jukes and parties of the Delta during Johnson's time. Essential.

Standout Track: "Smokes Like Lightning," giving us the earlier form of the later standard "Smokestack Lightnin'."

John Lee Hooker, *The Country Blues of John Lee Hooker*

Back in the late '50s, folk-blues was starting to be all the rage, and record companies wanted to cash in by giving their electric R&B artists acoustic guitars and recording the results. The story goes that for this 1959 session, Hooker was told to record a set of Lead Belly tunes. After responding that he'd never heard of Lead Belly, Hooker dug deep into his Delta repertoire and instead served up a sample what he would have sounded like in his acoustic troubadour days, with a set that ranges from Charley Patton ("Pony Blues") to the first Sonny Boy Williamson ("Good Morning Lil' School Girl") and Leroy Carr ("How Long Blues," a tune that Lead Belly also covered). A fascinating glimpse into what the music in the pre-war Delta jukes might have sounded like.

Standout Track: The modal Delta sounds of "Church Bell Tone."

Ry Cooder, *Crossroads* **OST**

The official soundtrack to the Ralph Macchio vehicle. What it lacks in Steve Vai it more than makes up for in Ry Cooder sliding, Sonny Terry whoopin', and a stunning recreation of authentic Delta sounds updated for '80s audiences.

Standout Track: "Feelin' Bad Blues," sad and slow slide guitar at its finest.

John Hammond, *At The Crossroads: The Blues of Robert Johnson*

John Hammond Jr. is a man with serious pedigree: His father John Hammond Sr. not only helped discover Benny Goodman, Bessie Smith, Bob Dylan, Bruce Springsteen, and Steve Ray Vaughan, to name just a small sample, but also arranged the *From Spirituals to Swing* concert and guided the release of the *King of the Delta Blues Singers* LP. John Hammond Jr. has dedicated his life to exploring the blues from the inside. This LP collects Hammond's interpretations of Johnson's music released on various LPs recorded between 1965 and 1978. The results range from the studiously authentic to electric rave-ups that give us a hint as to what Johnson might have sounded like if he'd lived long enough to go to Chicago in the electric blues boom of the '50s.

Standout Track: "Judgment Day" turns "If I Had Possession" into an electric juke joint rave-up.

The Peter Green Splinter Group, *Hot Foot Powder*

A John Mayall alumnus and founding member of Fleetwood Mac, Peter Green was one of those unfortunate few for whom the overused moniker "a troubled soul" is a perfectly accurate description. Green long held an affinity for Johnson's music—Fleetwood Mac's interpretation of "Hellhound on My Trail" stands out as a unique and powerful interpretation—and his '90s comeback with the Splinter Group included two albums dedicated entirely to Johnson's songs. This second album is the best of the two: Green is more confident in his playing, and he is ably assisted by some folks who know a thing or two about tackling the style, including Otis Rush, Dr. John, and Honeyboy Edwards.

Standout Track: "Little Queen of Spades" with guest Otis Rush drawing a straight line from Mississippi to the West Side of Chicago.

APPENDIX C: A Robert Johnson Timeline

1911:

May 8: Robert Johnson born in Hazlehurst, Mississippi

1929:

February 17: Johnson marries Virginia Travis.

1930:

April 10: Virginia Travis dies in childbirth.

1931:

May 4: Johnson marries Callie Craft.

1936:

November 23 to 27: Johnson's first recording sessions, San Antonio, Texas

1937:

June 19 and 20: Johnson's second recording sessions, Dallas, Texas

1938:

August 16: Death of Robert Johnson

December 23: The *From Spirituals to Swing* concert, featuring the disembodied, recorded voice of Robert Johnson, takes place at Carnegie Hall.

1941:

May 28: Georgia blues musician Frank Edwards records a version of "Terraplane Blues" for the Okeh label.

August 24: Alan Lomax makes his first recordings with Muddy Waters at the Stovall Plantation, just outside Clarksdale, Mississippi.

1948:

September: Muddy Waters records his version of "Kind Hearted Woman" for the Aristocrat label in Chicago. The recording was unissued until the 1967 Chess LP *More Real Folk Blues*.

1951:

August 5: Elmore James records his rendition of "Dust My Broom," featuring Rice Miller, the second Sonny Boy Williamson, on the blues harp. The record's amplified Delta sounds set the tone for Elmore's career and for the era of electric blues.

1959:

Sam Charters releases the book *The Country Blues*, one of the first major studies on the rural blues tradition. A chapter of the book is dedicated to Johnson. Johnson's "Preachin' Blues (Up Jumped The Devil)" is also featured on the companion LP.

1961:

King of the Delta Blues Singers is released, making Johnson's music easily available for the first time

1965:

March 22: Bob Dylan releases *Bringing It All Back Home*, his first LP to feature electric instruments. A copy of *King of the Delta Blues Singers* can be seen prominently on the LP cover art.

1966:

March: The short-lived studio group Eric Clapton and the Powerhouse, featuring Eric, Jack Bruce, Steve Winwood, Manfred Mann's Pete York, and the obscure Ben Palmer on piano, records the first known blues-rock version of "Cross Road Blues."

July: The godfather of British Blues, John Mayall, releases his *Bluesbreakers featuring Eric Clapton* LP. The record reaches #6 in the U.K. album charts. As well as hipping a generation onto the sounds of Chicago blues, the LP features a version of "Ramblin' on My Mind" (featuring Clapton on vocals), which pushes Johnson's music firmly into the mainstream.

1968:

August 9: Cream's *Wheels of Fire* album is released, including their version of "Cross Road Blues," re-titled "Crossroads," and featuring Eric Clapton on lead guitar and vocals. The song reaches #28 in the U.S.

1969:

December 5: The Rolling Stones release the LP *Let It Bleed*, featuring their cover of "Love In Vain," previously uncompiled and available only on bootlegs and rare 78 rpm records.

1970:

King of the Delta Blues Singers Vol. II released, including many of Johnson's songs better known through renditions by other artists, such as "Dust My Broom," "Sweet Home Chicago," and "Love in Vain."

1975:

Greil Marcus's book *Mystery Train* is released. Marcus presents Johnson as part of the story of rock and roll, a precursor to figures such as Elvis Presley and Sly Stone. The Crossroads myth is central to Marcus's telling. The book is quickly hailed as a classic and has become one of the defining texts of rock criticism.

APPENDIX C: A ROBERT JOHNSON TIMELINE

1986:

January 23: The first group of inductees is inducted into the Rock and Roll Hall of Fame. In addition to authentic rockers such as Elvis Presley, Chuck Berry, Buddy Holly, and Jerry Lee Lewis, Johnson is included as an "early influence," along with "Singing Brakeman" Jimmie Rodgers and boogie pianist Jimmy Yancey.

March 14: Release of the film *Crossroads*. Starring Ralph Macchio and featuring a soundtrack by Ry Cooder, the film received middling reviews and was a commercial failure. Despite this, the film plays an important role in establishing Robert Johnson and the story of the Crossroads in the mainstream, paving the way for the release of Johnson's *Complete Recordings*.

1990:

August 28: *The Complete Recordings* box set is released. Originally pressed in low numbers and expected to be sold mostly to collectors and specialists, the release ends up going platinum, selling more than a million copies.

1994:

September 17: The U.S. postal service issues a postage stamp featuring Johnson. Based on the "photo booth" picture, artistic license and social pressures mean that the photo-booth background was replaced with a more rural wooden wall and the cigarette dangling out of Johnson's mouth was absent.

1999:

May 11: Erection of the Crossroads monument in Clarksdale

2000:

October 19: The Coen Brothers' film *O Brother, Where Art Thou* is released. A critical and financial success, the film features blues musician Chris Thomas-King playing the part of Tommy Johnson, encountering the film's protagonist the morning after his Crossroads deal.

2006:

February 8: Robert Johnson is awarded a Lifetime Achievement Grammy.

2008:

November: *Vanity Fair* publishes a photo purported to show Robert Johnson and Johnny Shines. The photo's authenticity is disputed by blues scholars; however, it is claimed as authentic by the Johnson estate based on the evidence of forensic artist Lois Gibson.

2011:

The Robert Johnson Centennial Collection is released, building on *The Complete Recordings* with a re-ordered track listing, vastly improved sound, and an additional take of "Traveling Riverside Blues."

2013:

Another photo purported to show Johnson is unearthed. Found in an antique desk purchased by retired lawyer Donald Roark, the photo supposedly depicts Johnson, Callie Craft, Estella Coleman, and Robert Lockwood Jr. Rejected by *Living Blues* magazine, the photo eventually makes its way into the press and onto the internet. Once again, Lois Gibson has claimed the photograph as authentic.

2015:

June 30: Death of Claud Johnson

2020:

May 20: A verified third photo of Johnson is published in *Vanity Fair*. Taken at a photo booth on Beale Street, Memphis, and kept in the personal possessions of Robert's stepsister, Annye C. Anderson, the picture shows a smiling figure, proudly showing off his guitar, and offers no hints of devilry, tragedy, or diabolic deals.

REFERENCES

BIBLIOGRAPHY

Armstrong, Karen, *A Short History of Myth*, Melbourne, Canongate, 2005

Arp, Robert (ed), *The Devil and Philosophy: The Nature of His Game*, Chicago, Open Court, 2014

Bebergal, Peter, *Season of the Witch: How the Occult Saved Rock and Roll*, New York, Penguin, 2014

Beaumont, Daniel, *Preachin' the Blues: The Life and Times of Son House*, Oxford, Oxford University Press, 2011

Birnbaum, Larry, *Before Elvis: The Prehistory of Rock 'n' Roll.* Lanham, Massachusetts: Scarecrow Press, 2012

Black, Jason S; Hyatt, Christopher S, *Pacts With The Devil* (Third Edition), Reno, New Falcon Publications, 2009

Bloomfield, Michael, *Me and Big Joe,* V/Search, 1999

Bogdanov, Vladmir; Woodstra, Chris; Erlewhine, Stephen Tomas (eds), *All Music Guide to the Blues* (3rd edition), Backbeat Books, 2003

Booth, Stanley, *Rhythm Oil*, New York, Pantheon Books, 1981

Brown, Cecil, *Stagolee Shot Billy*, Cambridge, Harvard University Press, 2003

Butler, E.M, *The Myth of the Magus*, Cambridge, Canto, 1993

Campbell, Joseph, *The Hero with A Thousand Faces*, London, Fontana Press, 1993

Campbell, Joseph, *The Power of Myth*, New York, Anchor Books, 1991

Cavendish, Richard, *The Black Arts*, New York, Tarcher Perigee, 2017

Canizaras, Baba Raul, *Eshu-Eleggua Elegbara: Santeria and the Orisha of the Crossroads*, New York, Original Publications, 2000

Charters, Sam, *The Country Blues*, New York, Da Capo Press, 1975

Charters, Sam, *Robert Johnson*. Oak Publications, 1973

Cohen, Rich, *The Record Men: Chess Records and the Birth of Rock & Roll*, London, Profile Books, 2005

Combs, Allan; Holland, Mark, *Synchronicity: Through the Eyes of Science, Myth and The Trickster*, New York, Marlow, 2001

Conforth, Bruce; Wardlow, Gayle Dean, *Up Jumped the Devil: The Real Life of Robert Johnson*, Omnibus Press, 2019

Conforth Bruce, *Ike Zimmerman: The X in Robert Johnson's Crossroads*, 2008, Living Blues 194

Cosentino, Donald, *Who Is That Fellow in the Many-Colored Cap? Transformations of Eshu in Old and New World Mythologies*, 1987, The Journal of American Folklore, Vol. 100, No. 397

Copenhaver, Brian, *The Book of Magic: From Antiquity to the Enlightenment*, London, Penguin Books, 2016

Davis, Rebecca, *Blind Owl Blues: The Mysterious Life and Death of Blues Legend Alan Wilson*, Blind Owl Blues, 2013

d'Este, Sorita; Rankine, David, *Hekate Liminal Rites*, London, Avalonia, 2009

Dimech, A; Grey, P; Stratton-Kent, J (eds), *At The Crossroads*, Scarlet Imprint, 2012

Dryendal, Asbjorn; Lewis, James R; Peterson, Jesper AA, *The Invention of Satanism*, Oxford, Oxford University Press, 2016

Dylan, Bob, *Chronicles Vol 1*, New York, Simon and Schuster, 2004

Edwards, David Honeyboy, *The World Don't Owe Me Nothing: The Life and Times of Delta Bluesman Honeyboy Edwards*, Chicago Review Press, 1997

Elliade, Mircea, *A History of Religious Ideas*, tr W Trask, Chicago, University of Chicago Press, 1978-1985, 3 vols

Evans, Mike, *Ray Charles: The Birth of Soul*, Omnibus Press, 2007

Filan, Kenaz, *The New Orleans Voodoo Handbook*, Rochester, Destiny Books, 2011

Flowers, Stephen E, *Lords of the Left Hand Path, Forbidden Practices and Spiritual Heresies From the Cult of Set to the Church of Satan*, Rochester, Inner Traditions, 2012

Franz, Steve, *The Amazing Secret History of Elmore James,* Tuscon, BlueSource Publications, 2003

Gioia, Ted, *Delta Blues: The Life and Times of the Mississippi Masters Who Revolutionized American Music*, New York, W. W. Norton, 2008

Goethe, Johann Wolfgang von, *Faust Part One* (tr Wayne, Philip), London, Penguin Books, 1949

Goethe, Johann Wolfgang von, *Faust Part Two* (tr Wayne, Philip), London, Penguin Books, 1959

Gordon, Robert, *Can't Be Satisfied: The Life and Times of Muddy Waters*, London, Random House, 2003

Gordon, Robert, *Memphis Rent Party*, New York, Bloomsbury, 2019

Gosden, Chris, *The History of Magic from Alchemy to Witchcraft, from the Ice Age to the Present*, London, Penguin Books, 2020

Graves, Tom, *Crossroads: The Life and Afterlife of Blues Legend Robert Johnson* (second edition), Memphis, Rhythm Oil Publications, 2012

Guralnick, Peter, *Searching for Robert Johnson*, New York, Plume, 1998

Guralnick, Peter, *Sam Phillips: The Man Who Invented Rock 'n' Roll*, London, Weidenfeld & Nicolson, 2015

Gussow, Adam, *Beyond the Crossroads: The Devil and the Blues Tradition*, Chapel Hill, The University of North Carolina Press, 2017

Hamilton, Marybeth, *In Search of the Blues: Black Voices, White Visions*, Jonathan Cape, 1997

Handy, W.C., *Father of the Blues*, New York, Macmillan, 1941

REFERENCES

Hoodoo Sen Moise, *Working Conjure: A Guide to Hoodoo Folk Magic*, Newburyport, Weiner Books, 2018

Horowitz, Mitch, *Occult America: White House Seances, Ouija Circles, Masons, and the Secret Mystic History of Our Nation*, New York, Bantam, 2010

Howe, Katherine (ed.), *The Penguin Book of Witches*, London, Penguin Books, 2014

Hurston, Zora Neale, *Hoodoo In America*, Journal of American Folklore, XLIV (1931), p 358

Hyatt, Harry Middleton, *Hoodoo - Conjuration - Witchcraft - Rootwork: Beliefs Accepted By Many Negroes and White Persons These Being Orally Recorded Among Blacks and Whites*, Hannibal, West Pub, 1970

Hyde, Lewis, *Trickster Makes This World: How Disruptive Imagination Creates Culture*, Edinburgh, Canongate, 2008

Johnston, Sarah Iles, *Hekate Soteira: A Study of Hekate's Roles in the Chaldean Oracles and Related Literature*, Oxford University Press, 1990

Kail, Tony, *A Secret History of Memphis Hoodoo: Rootworkers, Conjurors and Spirituals*, Charleston, The History Press, 2017

Kail, Tony, *Stories of Rootworkers and Hoodoo in the Mid-South*, Charleston, The History Press, 2019

King, Chris Thomas, *The Blues: the Authentic Narrative of My Music and Culture*, Chicago, Chicago Review Press, 2021

Kramer, Heinrich, *Malleus Maleficarum*, tr Montague Summers, Dover Books, 1971

Lauterbach, Preston, *The Chitlin' Circuit and the Road to Rock 'n' Roll*, New York, W.W. Norton, 2012

Leeming, David, *The Oxford Companion to World Mythology*, Oxford, Oxford University Press, 2005

Lomax, Alan, *The Land Where The Blues Began*, London, Minerva, 1994

Louv, Jason, *John Dee and the Empire of Angels: Enochian Magic and the Occult Roots of the Modern World*, Rochster, Living Traditions, 2018

Luckhurst, Roger, *Zombies: A Cultural History*, London, Reaktion Books, 2015

Marlowe, Christopher, *Doctor Faustus and Other Plays*, ed Bevington, David; Rasmussen, Eric, Oxford, Oxford University Press, 1995

Marcus, Geil, *Mystery Train: Images of America in Rock 'n' Roll Music*, New York, E.P. Dutton, 1975

Mezzo, Dupont, J.M, *Love in Vain: Robert Johnson, 1911-1938*, London, Faber & Faber, 2014

Mezzrow, Mezz; Wolf, Bernard, *Really The Blues*, New York, Random House, 1946

Miller, James, *Almost Grown: The Rise of Rock*, London, Arrow Books, 2000

Milward, John, *Crossroads: How the Blues Shaped Rock 'n' Roll (and Rock Saved the Blues)*, UPNE, 2013

Morgan, Mogg, *Seth and the Two Ways: Ways of Seeing the "Demon God" of Ancient Egypt*, Oxford, Mandrake of Oxford, 2019

Murray, Charles Shaar, *Boogie Man: The Adventures of John Lee Hooker in the American 20th Century*, Penguin, 1999

Murray, Charles Shaar, *Crosstown Traffic: Jimi Hendrix and the Rock 'n' Roll Revolution*, New York, St Martin's Press, 1989

Obrecht, Jas, *Ry Cooder – Talking Country Blues and Gospel*, Guitar Player, July 1990

Oliver, Paul, *Blues Fell this Morning: Meaning In The Blues*, Cambridge University Press. 1990

Palmer, Robert, *Deep Blues*, New York, Penguin Books, 1982

Pearson, Billy Lee and McCulloch, Bill, *Robert Johnson Lost and Found*, Urbana, University of Chicago Press, 2003

Pennick, Nigel, *Operative Witchcraft: Spellwork & Herbcraft in the British Isles*, Rochester, Destiny Books, 2019

Richards, Keith, *Life*, Hachette Australia, 2011

Romanowski, Patricia; George-Warren, Holly (eds), *The New Rolling Stone Encyclopedia of Rock & Roll*, New York, Fireside, 1995

Russell, Jeffrey Burton, *The Devil: Perceptions of Evil From Antiquity to Primitive Christianity*, Ithaca, Cornell University Press, 1977

Sacre, Robert (ed), *Charley Patton: Voice of the Mississippi Delta*, University Press of Mississippi, 2018

Schroder, Patricia R, *Robert Johnson: Mythmaking and Contemporary Culture*, Chicago, University of Illinois Press, 2004

Segal, Robert A, *Myth: A Very Short Introduction*, Oxford, Oxford University Press, 2004

Segrest, James; Hoffman, Mark, *Moanin' at Midnight: The Life and Times of Howlin' Wolf*, Da Capo Press, 2005

Standford, Peter, *The Devil: A Biography*, London, Mandarin, 1996

Sworder, Roger, *Science & Religion in Archaic Greece*, San Rafael, Sophia Perennis, 2008

Te Velde, H. *Seth, God of Confusion; A Study of His Rule in Egyptian Mythology and Religion*, Brill Archive, 1967

Te Velde, H. *The Egyptian God Seth as a Trickster*, Journal of the American Research Center in Egypt 7 (1968): 37-40

Thompson, Dave, *Bayou Underground: Tracing the Mythical Roots of American Popular Music*, Toronto, ECW Press, 2010

Titon, Jeff Todd, *Early Downhome Blues: A Musical and Cultural Analysis (Second Edition)*, The University of North Carolina Press, 1994

Virgil, *The Aeneid* (tr Fagles, Robert), London, Penguin Books, 2008

Wald, Elijah, *Escaping the Delta: Robert Johnson and the Invention of the Blues*, New York, HarperCollins, 2004

Wald, Elijah, *The Blues: A Very Short Introduction*, Oxford, Oxford University Press, 2010

Wardlow, Gayle Dean; Komara, Edward M., *Chasin' that Devil Music: Searching for the Blues*, San Francisco:.Miller Freeman Books, 1998

Webb, Don, *The Seven Faces of Darkness: Practical Typhonian Magic,* Bastrop, Runa-Raven Press, 1996

Wilson, Colin, *The Outsider*, London, Pan Books, 1963

Wyman, Bill, *Bill Wyman's Blues Odyssey: A Journey to Music's Heart and Soul,* London, DK, 2001

Yates, Frances, *The Occult Philosophy in the Elizabethan Age*, Abingdon, Oxon, Routledge, 2001

FILMOGRAPHY

Black Snake Moan, directed by Craig Brewer, Paramount, 2006

Crossroads, directed by Walter Hill, 1986, Columbia Pictures

Faust: Eine deutsche Volkssage, directed by F.W. Murnau, 1926

Petey Wheatstraw, directed by Cliff Roquemore, 1977, Comedian International Enterprises

Remastered: Devil at The Crossroads, directed by Brian Oakes, 2019, Netflix

Satan & Adam, directed by V. Scott Balcerek, 2018, Netflix

The Search For Robert Johnson, directed by Chris Hunt, 1991, Iambic Productions

You See Me Laughin': The Last of the Hill Country Bluesmen, directed by Mandy Stein, 2002, Journeyman Pictures

www.ingramcontent.com/pod-product-compliance
Lightning Source LLC
Chambersburg PA
CBHW022334300426
44109CB00040B/542